Compliments Of:

We [...] your new home
Cay & Carly

CAY&Carly

A Father-Daughter Team

Cay (858)231-2451
Cay@CayandCarlyHomes.com
Carly (858)231-6722
Carly@CayandCarlyHomes.com
www.CayandCarlyHomes.com

We are pleased to present you with *"The Beaches Of San Diego: Your Ultimate Guide To The Sun, Sand & Surf"*. This book is offered to help acquaint you with the beautiful beaches of San Diego, for it is there that you may discover the many facets of the ocean, and there you are allowed to shed the cares of everyday life. The sun will inevitably set and the tide will ultimately wash away your footprints, but in the end you will always have your memories of the beach. May this book serve as a memento of San Diego, California and our appreciation for your continued business and referrals.

RealLiving LIFESTYLES
INTEGRATED REAL ESTATE SERVICES

The Beaches Of
SAN DIEGO

The Beaches Of
SAN DIEGO
Your Ultimate Guide to the Sun, Sand and Surf

Written by Gia Lucy

Photography by
Peter Phan and Gia Lucy
with select photography by Mark Brautigam

Vista Pacifica Publishing Company
Dana Point, California

Credits

First published in the United States in 2008
by Vista Pacifica Publishing Company
P.O. Box 373
Dana Point, CA 92629
(949) 395-2878
www.vistapacifica-publishing.com

ISBN: 0-9679452-2-4
Library of Congress Control Number: 2007935030
First Edition
Printed in China

Design & Production: Robert Brocke
Editors: Richard J. Collins and Theresa Moos
Photography: Peter Phan and Gia Lucy,
with select photography Mark Bautigam

Although the author and publisher has made every effort to ensure
the accuracy of the information contained in this book, we assume no
responsibility for errors, inaccuracies, omissions, or any inconsistency
herein. Further, we assume no liability for any loss, injury, or inconvenience
sustained by any traveler as a result of information or advice contained in
The Beaches Of San Diego – *Your Ultimate Guide to the Sun, Sand and Surf.*

Acknowledgements

I am truly blessed to have a family who shares in my love for the beach and ocean. Thank you Eric, Nathan and Kailea for joining me on my adventures of discovering new beaches, surfing uncharted waters and playing smashball and volleyball on San Diego beaches. I love you all.

To my mother, Elaine Danson, thank you for bringing me to the beach as a child and imparting your love for the beach and ocean to me. You have given me many cherished memories like jumping the waves and digging my way to China.

To Bill and Karen Lucy, thank you for all of your encouragement and the countless hours of babysitting which enabled me to finish the book.

To Richard Collins, Herr Wundervoll, my grandfather and true friend, thank you for your wisdom guidance and encouragement.

To Peter Phan, once again you have come through with stunning photographs. They encompasses the grandeur and beauty of San Diego.

To Mark Brautiagam a true surfer, ocean lover and awesome photographer. Your stunning photographs breathe life and make this book come alive. I appreciate all your hard work. Thank you.

To Robert Brocke, once again your creative ways and hard work have garnered a masterful 'work of art'. You are talented and much appreciated.

"The Lord's loving kindnesses indeed never cease, For His compassions never fail. They are new every morning; Great is Thy faithfulness." — *Lamentations 3:22-23*

The Beaches Of SAN DIEGO

Table of Contents

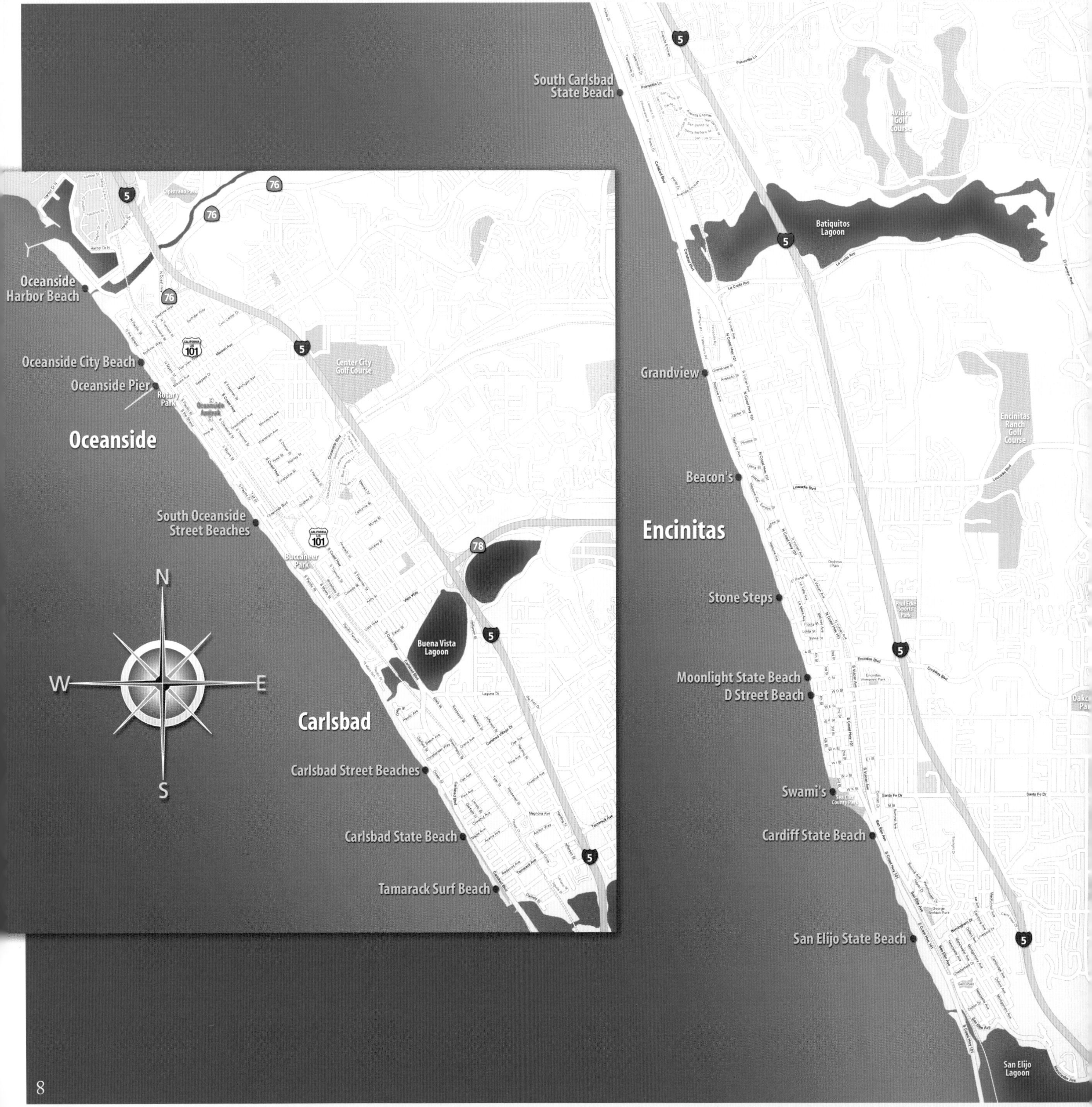

South Carlsbad
State Beach

Batiquitos
Lagoon

Oceanside
Harbor Beach

Oceanside City Beach

Oceanside Pier

Oceanside

Grandview

Beacon's

Encinitas

South Oceanside
Street Beaches

Stone Steps

Buena Vista
Lagoon

Moonlight State Beach
D Street Beach

Carlsbad

N

W   E

S

Carlsbad Street Beaches

Swami's

Cardiff State Beach

Carlsbad State Beach

Tamarack Surf Beach

San Elijo State Beach

San Elijo
Lagoon

Center City
Golf Course

Aviara
Golf
Course

Encinitas
Ranch
Golf
Course

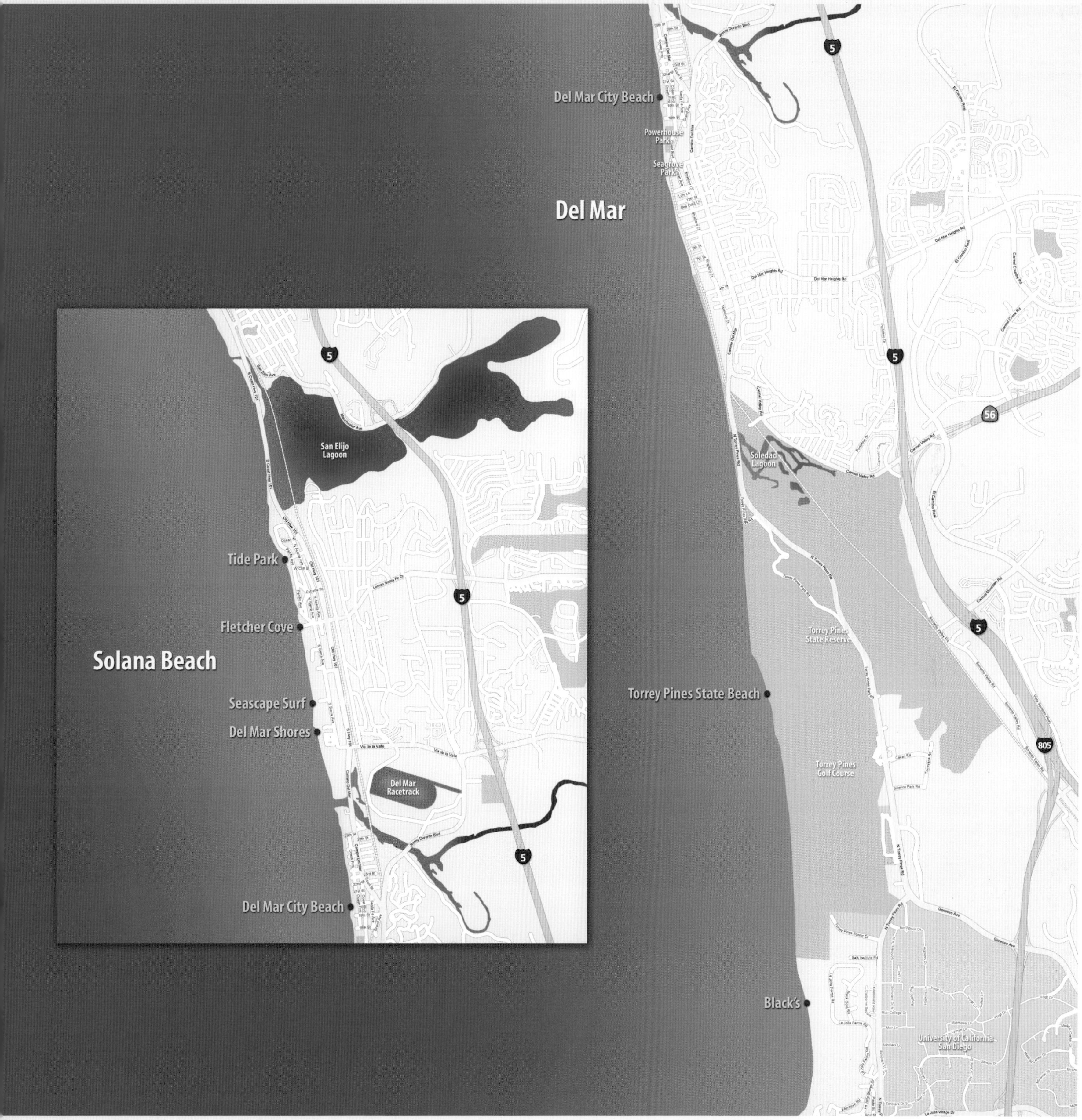

Del Mar

Del Mar City Beach

Powerhouse Park

Seagrove Park

Solana Beach

San Elijo Lagoon

Tide Park

Fletcher Cove

Seascape Surf

Del Mar Shores

Del Mar Racetrack

Del Mar City Beach

Soledad Lagoon

Torrey Pines State Reserve

Torrey Pines State Beach

Torrey Pines Golf Course

Black's

University of California, San Diego

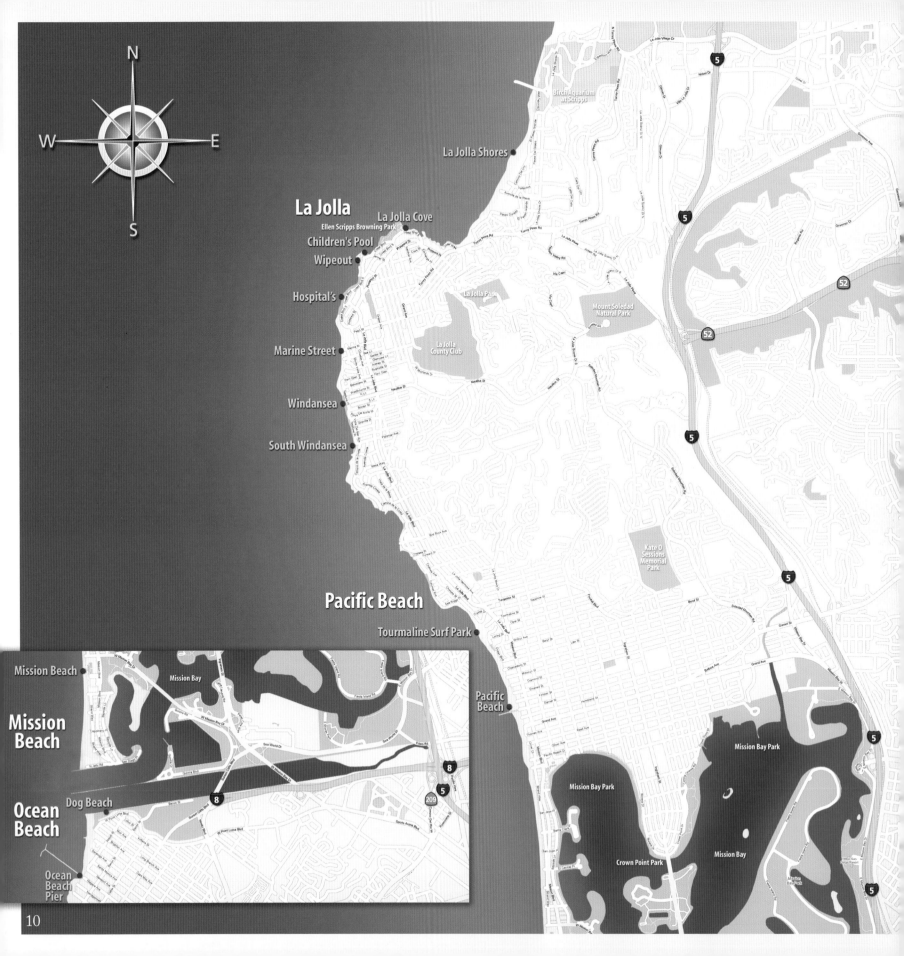

N
W E
S

La Jolla Shores •

La Jolla
Ellen Scripps Browning Park • La Jolla Cove
Children's Pool •
Wipeout •

Hospital's •

Marine Street •

Windansea •

South Windansea •

Birch Aquarium at Scripps

La Jolla Park

Mount Soledad Natural Park

La Jolla County Club

Kate O Sessions Memorial Park

Pacific Beach

Tourmaline Surf Park •

Pacific Beach •

Mission Bay Park

Mission Bay Park

Mission Bay

Crown Point Park

Mission Beach
Mission Beach •
Mission Bay

Ocean Beach
Dog Beach •

Ocean Beach Pier

Sea World Dr

75

5

Silver Strand State Beach

5

5

Bayfront Park

SDG&E Park Centennial Park

75

Tidelands Park

75

Coronado City Beach

Hotel Del Coronado

Coronado

75

Coronado Shores

Glorietta Bay Park

5

75

Palm Ave

Carnation Ave
Caña Ave
Citrus Ave
Palm Ave
Daisy Ave
Donax Ave
Date Ave
Elm Ave
Elder Ave
Evergreen Ave
Emory Ave
Ebony Ave
Encina Ave
Coronado Ave

Imperial Beach Pier

Imperial Beach Blvd

905

905

5

Otay Fwy

Imperial Beach

Tijuana River National Estuarine Reserve

Imperial Beach Pier

Monument Rd

Foreword

Close your eyes and think about your favorite beach. How does the sand feel between your toes? What time of day is it? What kind of sounds do you hear? Who are you with?

These simple reflections always bring a smile to my face and anticipation towards the next time I set foot in the sand. It's easy to see how everyone loves the beach - happy childhood memories are relived with each visit and there is a youthful sense of freedom that the salt air conjures up. Reinvigorate, reenergize, and relax – that is what a day at the beach can do for the soul.

In the pages of this book, Gia Lucy shares with you some of the loveliest beaches in the world. From world-class waves at Windansea to Imperial Beach's incredible coastal reserve, each place has its own special personality that Gia effectively captures. Which one is your favorite? Is it Oceanside's miles of beach breaks? Black's liberal clothing policy? La Jolla's crystal cove? Tourmaline's classic lines? The scene at Mission Beach? Coronado's old time allure? There are so many beaches in San Diego to choose from, you'll want to visit and explore all of them.

We are truly fortunate to be able to enjoy these beautiful beaches, and as such, we must make every effort to protect them for future generations. Our beaches are precious, natural resources treat them with special care. Take only your memories. Leave only your footprints.

Through this book Gia opens up the door for you to explore all that San Diego's beaches have to offer. Go for a swim, surf, dive, sail, paddle or soak in the warm sun. Visit as many San Diego beaches as you can, then decide for yourself which ones are your favorite.

Lia Colabello
International Relations Manager
Surfrider Foundation

The Beaches of San Diego

There are some experiences that invariably shape a person. For me, it was the first time I stood at the edge of the ocean mustering up the courage to throw myself in. That day still blissfully lingers in my memory. I dog-paddled out into the surf, was pushed by the whitewash and for a few sweet moments bobbed along in a cloud of meringue. From that very moment my adventurer's heart had been caught.

Swamis, Ocean Beach, Pacific Beach, Pipes, Beacons… these beaches were common, household names that I heard nearly everyday growing up. My three older brothers and dad, all avid surfers and fishermen, would recount their days at the beach surfing or fishing off the pier during dinner. I found myself daydreaming of those beaches.

As a teenager, my dreams became a reality. I spent every summer – from long-awaited Memorial Day to Labor Day – on the beach. I learned to surf at Offshore Beach; boogie boarded Oceanside Pier and snorkeled La Jolla Cove.

Now, as an adult, my brother, Kevin, and I go on what we call 'excursions'. We explore a 10-mile stretch of coast by walking, swimming, bodysurfing, rock climbing, cliff jumping and snorkeling the entire length. It began quite simply… I just wanted to see what was around the bend.

Eventually, I became one of those people who got tangled up in that ultimate dream of working at what you love. Even now, after completing my first book, *Sun, Sand & Surf – The Ultimate Guide To Orange County Beaches,* and having written, *The Beaches Of San Diego – Your Ultimate Guide To The Sun, Sand & Surf,* I am still romanced by the notion of a unexplored beach.

My hope is that this book will bring to readers the delight and even some of the passion for the beach and the ocean, which I still enjoy. And to inspire others to, as Mark Twain once said, "Throw off the bowlines. Sail away from the safe harbor. Catch the trade winds in your sails. Explore. Dream. Discover."

Introduction

San Diego, the second largest city in California and the sixth largest city in the nation, steadfastly retains the charm and appeal of a lively beach town amid a bustling international metropolis. Imagine a painter's canvas of wild deserts and rugged mountains gradually giving way to a sparkling city with towering

skyscrapers, shaded streets lined with outdoor cafes, cozily settled neighborhoods, honey colored beaches, marinas, piers and seaside villas - then sea to infinity. This is the picture of everyday life in San Diego. Combine this with a spirited surf culture, Mediterranean climate, friendly people and attractions like Historic Old Town, Balboa Park, The San Diego Zoo, Sea World, Lego Land, horse races, and the Del Mar Fair and its easy to understand why San Diego has earned its well-deserved reputation as one of the most popular beach and surf destinations in the country.

Eleven coastal cities – Oceanside, Carlsbad, Encinitas, Solana Beach, Del Mar, La Jolla,

Pacific Beach, Mission Beach, Ocean Beach, Coronado Island and Imperial Beach – border 41 sun-soaked strands. Like each coastal city, each San Diego beach possesses its own allure, attractions and unique personality. Each is equally as marvelous as the next, and all share the same beautiful sunset which each night transforms the sky into a blazing fire and the ocean into shimmering liquid gold. Still, there are certain things that beach lovers simply can't live without: wide open strands, frolicking surf, mom and pop taco stands, bonfire pits and beachside amusement parks. Whatever your interest, San Diego has a beach to suit your style.

For "Classic California" surf beaches, where locals ride waves with the nonchalant grace of rolling surf art, visit Tourmaline and Cardiff State Beach. For those looking for a perpetual beach party, join the parade of people at Pacific Beach or Ocean Beach Pier where you can rent kayaks, bikes or in-line skates to paddle, pedal or glide to your next beach bash destination. If spending hours with a mask strapped to your face and snorkel bobbing above the surface is your version of paradise, head to La Jolla Shores or La Jolla Cove to see gem-colored fish and sharks. Families can find an exciting array of activities for their young ones

at Moonlight and Oceanside Harbor Beach. From surfing and snorkeling to sunbathing and swimming, you'll find it all along San Diego's coast. So, don a bikini or a pair of board shorts, lather on the sunscreen, grab the beach gear and discover for yourself *The Beaches Of San Diego – Your Ultimate Guide To The Sun, Sand & Surf.*

Oceanside Harbor Beach

Beach Access: *Located along Harbor Drive South in Oceanside. Take the I-5 freeway to Oceanside and exit Harbor Drive, west. Harbor Drive will take you directly to the entrance of the Harbor. Turn left at the fork and follow the curving road to the paid parking lot.*
Beach Hours: *24 hours*

As June draws near and schools close their doors for summer recess, many families pack beach bags and surf gear and set off to Harbor Beach to begin their holiday.

This favorite vacation destination for ocean-loving families is framed by tall palms and two jetties, where kids can fish for corbina, opal eye and halibut. It is a place which affords families the opportunity to abandon the car and enjoy a seaside retreat complete with almost all the ingredients that make for a memorable family trip: body surfing, bodyboarding, body-thumping waves, mom and pop pizza parlor, an oceanfront open-air Mc Donald's, an ice cream shop, bonfire rings, picnic tables, playground, and souvenir boutiques.

Oceanside Harbor Beach

For families who wish to stay overnight and experience Oceanside Harbor's wildlife, bring the R.V and camp out at the R.V. campground at the north end of the beach, or settle in at one of the cozy oceanfront vacation rentals at the south end. Wake up early and rent a motorboat, sailboat or kayak and ply the waters in search of dolphins and whales. Or, to better your odds at spying marine animals, book an excursion on a sportsfishing or whale-watching boat.

Whether you come for the day or overnight, you are almost certain to discover the family charm of this Cape Cod styled harbor and strand.

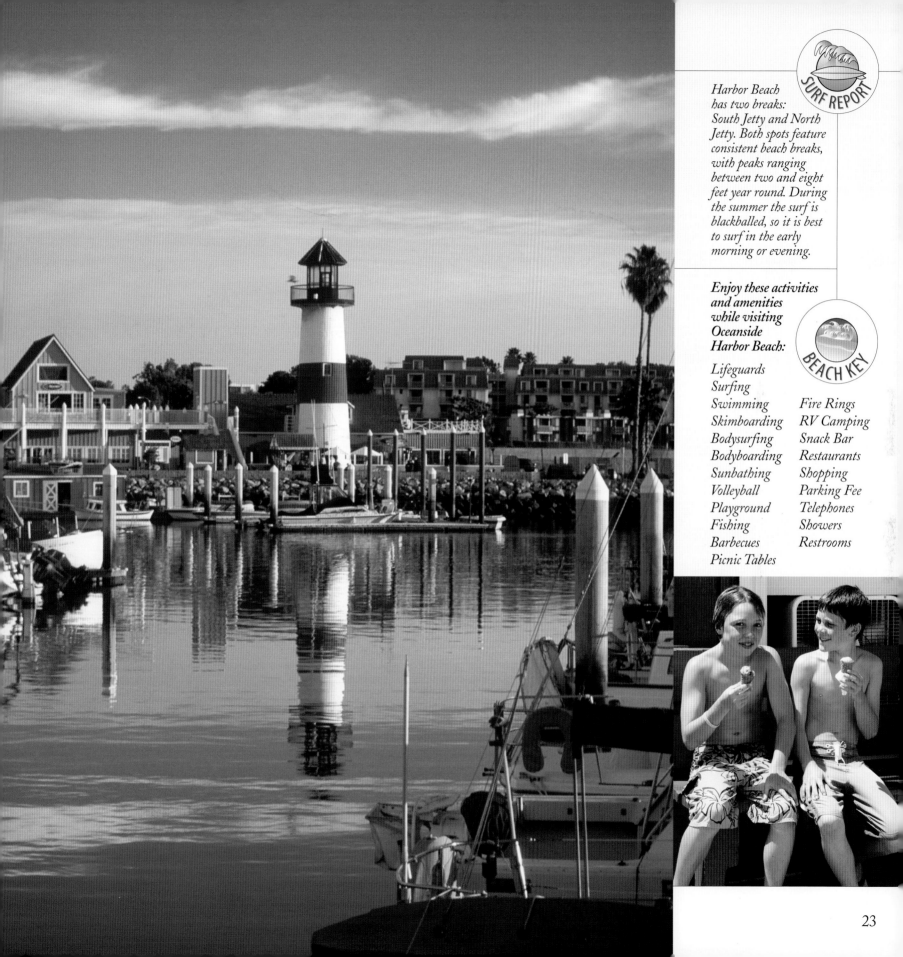

Harbor Beach has two breaks: South Jetty and North Jetty. Both spots feature consistent beach breaks, with peaks ranging between two and eight feet year round. During the summer the surf is blackballed, so it is best to surf in the early morning or evening.

Enjoy these activities and amenities while visiting Oceanside Harbor Beach:

Lifeguards	
Surfing	
Swimming	*Fire Rings*
Skimboarding	*RV Camping*
Bodysurfing	*Snack Bar*
Bodyboarding	*Restaurants*
Sunbathing	*Shopping*
Volleyball	*Parking Fee*
Playground	*Telephones*
Fishing	*Showers*
Barbecues	*Restrooms*
Picnic Tables	

23

Oceanside City Beach

Beach Access: *Traveling north or south along the I-5 freeway exit Mission Avenue, west. Turn right onto North Myers Street. Park along the residential streets at the meters, and walk down to the beach.* **Beach Hours:** *24 hours*

S et between the energy and hubbub of Oceanside Harbor Beach and Oceanside Pier, Oceanside City Beach is an ideal respite for those wishing to be away from the crowds but close enough to enjoy the amenities and attractions offered at both beaches.

At Oceanside City Beach, enjoy sunning under the swaying palms that line the promenade, or watching the boats with their whitewashed sails billowing against the technicolor-blue sky, or dozing off to the sound of the ocean's waves only to be awakened by flocks of birds flying so low that the beat of their wings stir up the sand.

When you are ready for a little more action, join the locals in an impromptu soccer match or volleyball game. Then follow the parade of cyclists and in-line skaters along the Strand to the Oceanside Pier, where a summer concert and sunset serves as a perfect complement to a relaxing day.

SURF REPORT

The 3.5 miles that make up Oceanside's beaches, for the most part, all feature typical beach breaks. Oceanside City beach follows suite. Sandbars create a typical beach break that works best on a south to southwest swell and blows out in the early afternoon.

BEACH KEY

Enjoy these activities and amenities while visiting Oceanside City Beach:

Lifeguards
Surfing
Swimming
Bodysurfing
Bodyboarding
Skimboarding
Skate & Bike Trails
Sunbathing
Volleyball
Pinic Tables
Fire Rings
Surf Fishing
Showers
Restrooms
Parking Fee

Oceanside Pier

Beach Access: *Located along Mission Ave and Pacific Street in Oceanside. Traveling along Highway 101, turn west onto Mission Avenue. Turn Left onto North Pacific Street. Park at the paid parking lot and walk to the beach.* **Beach Hours:** *24 hours*

A palm-tree-lined promenade called The Strand where beachgoers zip along on bikes, roller blades and scooters gives way to Oceanside Pier and beach, which in the summer becomes a favorite stomping ground for many Oceanside residents. This family-oriented beach and pier offers so many different activities that your crew is almost certain to be off and running the moment their feet reach the sand. With options such as surfing and bodyboarding to fishing and playing basketball in the community center's indoor courts, it seems that the only dilemma is deciding which to do first.

One solution is to start the day off early with breakfast at the 1950's styled diner, situated at the end of the pier. If the 1,942-foot walk seems a bit daunting - without your morning's coffee - then hop aboard the shooby dooby shuttle and for a buck you'll be whisked to the end of the pier and will be enjoying a cup of joe in no time flat. Save your leftovers for the stroll back along the pier where plenty of hungry birds perched along the railings will sing, swoop and fly for a free handout.

Oceanside Pier

Next, plant yourself on the beach and relax as your children take in summer's simplest pleasures: playing at the playground, frolicking in the waves, and constructing cities out of sand.

Later, cast a weighted line into the water, then watch as fleeting gray shadows nibble gently on the bait, then bite and wait to be reeled in. In all actuality, catching fish may not be as simple as this sounds, but it carries us away from the routine of everyday life and allows us to concentrate on what is really important: reeling in a mammoth-sized fish so you can get your picture on the fisherman's board of fame.

On a solid south to southwest swell, Oceanside Pier's waves break thick and hollow. Surfing during a morning session at low tide is optimal since the afternoon brings onshore winds that create flat or choppy conditions.

BEACH KEY

Enjoy these activities and amenities while visiting **Oceanside Pier Beach**:

Lifeguards
Surfing
Swimming
Bodysurfing
Bodyboarding
Skimboarding
Playground
Basketball
Fishing
Fishing Pier
Fire Rings
Skate & Bike Trails
Snack Bar
Restaurants
Train Depot
Showers
Restrooms
Parking Fee

29

South Oceanside Street Beaches

Beach Access: *Located along Pacific Street in Oceanside. Take the I-5 freeway, exit Pacific Coast Highway. Turn west onto Cassidy Street. Turn right onto Pacific Street. Park along Pacific Street at one of the following streets: Tyson, Wisconsin, Forester, Oceanside Boulevard, Buccaneer and Cassidy.* **Beach Hours:** *24 hours*

Just south of the Oceanside Pier lies a series of free-parking beaches accessible from Pacific Street. Six beaches - Tyson, Wisconsin, Forester, Oceanside Boulevard, Buccaneer and Cassidy - collectively form South Oceanside Street Beaches.

This long, narrow strand, backed by weathered vacation cottages with picket fences and small porches – which peer out onto a blue sweep of ocean – imparts vacationers with a sense of endless summer, filled with promises of adventure and relaxation.

All beaches lead to the same strand but each caters to a slightly different crowd. Tyson Street finds teenagers sunning themselves along the grassy knoll situated above the shore, and children clambering up and down as they play on the equipment at the park.

At Wisconsin Street, vacationers make the most of their vacation rental's backyard: the seashore. Couples stroll along the water's edge drinking their morning coffee. And once the sun warms the strand, they tuck a boogie board under their arms and set out to ride the waves.

Forester, Oceanside Boulevard and Buccaneer Beach are outfitted for families. Each beach features designated

swim and surf areas where parents and children can enjoy skimboarding, bodyboarding and surfing. Plus, at Buccaneer Beach, your kids will get a kick out of the small bridge that features cutouts of two-dimensional colorful fish and beach-goers toting surfboards – they almost look real! Make sure to visit the park situated behind the beach where you will find a snack bar, barbeques, play equipment, and a basketball court with two slate wood benches for spectators.

The last public beach access in Oceanside brings visitors to Cassidy Street. This section of strand is unlike the other 3.7 miles of beach due to the fact that it is made up of cobblestones rather than the soft, brown sand characteristic of neighboring beaches. This is the beach that many Oceanside locals claim to be their favorite.

On any given morning when the offshore winds begin to blow, many of North County's surfers make their way to one of South Oceanside's Street Beaches for clean and hollow surf. These beaches break best on a south swell at low to medium tide.

Enjoy these activities and amenities while visiting **South Oceanside Street Beaches:**

BEACH KEY

Lifeguards
Surfing
Swimming
Bodyboarding
Skimboarding
Bodysurfing
Sunbathing
Playground
Basketball
Park
Barbecues
Snack Bar
Restrooms

33

CHAPTER TWO

Carlsbad

Carlsbad Street Beaches

Beach Access: *Located along Ocean Street in Carlsbad. Traveling along Highway 101, turn west onto Oak Avenue. Turn right onto Ocean Street. Park along Ocean Street and take any of the following stairways to the beach: Garfield, Beech, Christiansen, Grand Avenue, Carlsbad Village Drive. To reach Oak Avenue, turn left onto Ocean Street, park in the lot and scramble down the cliff to the beach.* **Beach Hours:** *6:00am – 11:00pm*

Six beach accesses – Garfield, Beech, Christiansen, Grand Avenue, Carlsbad Village Drive and Oak Avenue – make up Carlsbad Street Beaches.

Visitors can park along the residential streets and take one of five marked stairways down to the strand, or park in the lot at Oak Avenue and scramble down the short sandstone bluff to the beach. Either way visitors will find themselves along the same long and lovely caramel-colored sandy beach, which is backed by ornate four-story homes, vacation rentals and quaint hotels.

There is almost always a slight breeze which fans the shore at Carlsbad Street Beaches, making it an ideal place to set sail to a kite, and watch as it dances above the glittering Pacific.

The south end of the beach, known by locals as Offshore Beach, is where the regulars soak up the warm California rays and paddle out into the crashing surf.

On the north end of the beach, vacationers greet the day by reading the morning paper and watching the locals skim down the faces of 5-foot crashing waves on surfboards and bodyboards – perhaps paying close attention in hopes of learning a few techniques before testing their own agility in a private surf lesson offered by many local surf shops in town.

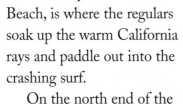

SURF REPORT

Carlsbad Street Beaches feature a typical California beach break, with good waves for learning how to surf. The best waves break on a south to southwest swell.

Enjoy these activities and amenities while visiting Carlsbad Street Beaches:

BEACH KEY

Lifeguards
Swimming
Surfing
Skimboarding
Bodyboarding
Kite Flying
Sunbathing
Shopping
Restaurants

Carlsbad State Beach

Beach Access: *Located along Carlsbad Blvd. in Carlsbad. Take the I-5 freeway and exit Carlsbad Village Drive, west. Turn left on to Carlsbad Blvd. Park along the highway at Tamarack and walk down the stairs or ramp to the beach.* **Beach Hours:** *6:00am – 10:00pm*

If there ever were a beach made for walkers and joggers, Carlsbad State beach, also known as John C. Frazee State Beach, would be it.

This famous walking beach features a 4,400-foot beachside paved pathway, appropriately named The Seawalk, as well as an equal length bluff-top boardwalk complete with picnic tables and vista points.

Stretching from Carlsbad State Beach to Agua Hedionda Lagoon, the structure was initially created as a solution to the shoreline erosion problem, but locals and visitors tend to be more enamored with its recreational uses than its conservation efforts.

On any given day, Carlsbad residents picnic at the bluff-top tables, new moms stroll their babies, surfers check the waves, senior citizens shuffle along the path enjoying the salt air, and physical fitness lovers keep an eye out for breaching whales while getting in their afternoon workout.

To be fair, Carlsbad State beach is not only ideal for walkers and joggers; it is also an excellent beach for ocean-loving families. During the summer, the strand is crowded with beach umbrellas, toys and chairs. The younger children entertain themselves by jumping the waves, while the older teens and adults bodyboard or surf at the favored breaks, Terramar and Tamarack Surf Beach.

Ocean-loving families enjoy bodyboarding and surfing at Carlsbad State Beach. Like most other beaches in North County, it works best on a south to southwest swell. For better surfing waves walk south to Tamarack Surf Beach.

Enjoy these activities and amenities while visiting Carlsbad State Beach:

Lifeguards
Swimming
Surfing
Sunbathing
Skimboarding
Bodysurfing
Bodyboarding
Sand Castle Building
Walking Trail
Picnic Tables
Shopping
Restaurants
Restrooms
Public Showers

Tamarack Surf Beach

Beach Access: *Located along Carlsbad Boulevard and Tamarack Avenue in Carlsbad. Take the I-5 freeway and exit Carlsbad Village Drive, west. Turn left onto Carlsbad Boulevard. Turn right into the lot at Tamarack Avenue and walk to the beach.*
Beach Hours: *6:00am – 10:00pm*

S urfing is not just a sport in Carlsbad; it's a way of life. And at Tamarack Surf Beach, it is a long-standing local tradition – one that is embraced with as much vigor and gusto as a Friday night high school football game. Everyone here loves surfing, young and old alike. Indeed, one of its charms is its communal appeal, which cuts across all boundaries of gender, class and age.

Be it a cool day in winter or a warm day in summer, if the reef or jetties are breaking the locals are out in the water surfing or on the shore observing. Families arrive with beach blankets, camera, sunscreen and boards in tow, to spend the day surfing with their loved ones.

One weekend a year, Tamarack Surf Beach is transformed from a surfers' haven into a seaside celebration and festival featuring arts and craft booths, jugglers, clowns and magicians for the kids, food vendors, 3-on-3 basketball tournaments, a classic car parade, a Hawaiian dance show, and a women's surf contest – all centered around the annual Carlsbad Triathlon. Ranking as the world's top five longest running triathlons, the race includes a 1k swim, 25k bike ride and a 5k run that begins at Tamarack Surf Beach and follows the coastline past Sand Diego's beautiful beaches, lagoons and a wildlife preserve. The whole town turns out to watch the race and enjoy the festivities.

SURF REPORT

For Carlsbad residents, who like to surf in their home town, Tamarack Surf Beach is the best bet. Smooth peaks break over an underwater reef forming fun, ridable waves up to six feet. Anything larger than six feet walls off.

BEACH KEY

Enjoy these activities and amenities while visiting Tamarack Surf Beach:

Lifeguards
Surfing
Bodyboarding
Sunbathing
Fishing
Restrooms

South Carlsbad State Beach

Beach Access: *Located along Carlsbad Boulevard and Poinsettia in Carlsbad. From the I-5 Freeway exit Poinsettia, west. Cross over Carlsbad Boulevard and enter the State Beach. Traveling along Highway 101, the Pacific Coast Highway turns into Carlsbad Boulevard. Entrance to the park is only accessible traveling southbound.*
Beach Hours: *6:00am – 10:00pm* Reservation Info: *(800) 444-7275*

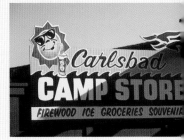

For every surfer or beach-lover who suffers from the affliction of having most of his or her conscious thoughts about the ocean, there's nothing quite as wondrous as falling asleep to the sound of crashing waves, under a kaleidoscope of stars, only to awake at dawn, fire-up a camp-style breakfast of bacon and eggs and then surf perfect, glassy waves. All this and more is possible at South Carlsbad State Beach.

Set on an aerie, high above the sparkling Pacific, the campgrounds often sleep tent flap to tent flap in the summer. The shores are crowded with large family groups picnicking, playing Frisbee, and learning to surf the old-fashioned way: through trial and error. But, visit in early

fall, when summer vacationers return to their school schedules and you'll find an almost empty seashore paved with sea glass, broken shells, and cobblestones.

For those who would like to visit South Carlsbad State Beach, but do not wish to stay overnight, park at the South Carlsbad State park North Ponto lot, located just south of Solamar Drive off Highway 101, or along the Pacific Coast Highway at Ponto Beach, located at the south end of South Carlsbad State Beach. Both accesses bring beach-goers to the same six-and-a half-mile beach strand, but are designed for day-use visitors.

South Carlsbad State Beach's slow, mushy waves and soft sandy floor make it an excellent place for beginning surfers and longboarders. For more experienced surfers or surf kayakers, head south to Ponto where better waves break just north of, or in between, the two jetties.

Enjoy these activities and amenities while visiting South Carlsbad State Beach:

BEACH KEY

Lifeguards
Swimming
Surfing
Skimboarding
Bodysurfing
Bodyboarding
Kayaking
Visitor Center
Tent Camping
R.V. Camping
Camp Store
Showers
Restrooms
Parking Fee

45

CHAPTER THREE

Encinitas

Grandview

Beach Access: *Located along Neptune Ave. in Encinitas. Take the I-5 freeway, exit La Costa Ave., west. Turn left on N. Coast Hwy. Turn left onto Grandview Ave. Turn right onto Neptune Avenue. Park free along the residential streets or in the lot.* **Beach Hours:** *5:00am – 10:00pm*

I n the parking lot directly opposite the stairway of Grandview beach, surfers greet one another with a quick nod of the head, towel change into trunks and wetsuits,

wax their boards, and then without hesitation make their way down the long, steep stairway to the beach – slowing only as they round the corner for the second and third flights of stairs.

Grandview beach is unique. Where else would you find all of the beachgoers in the water surfing and bodyboarding and not one person on the shore sunbathing beneath a perfect Crayola blue sky? The explanation is really quite simple: the

strand, a thin stretch of sand sandwiched between the ocean and steep eroding cliffs, is so narrow that the waves often cover the entire section and force unwary visitors dangerously close to the unstable bluffs. For sunbathing and other on-shore activities, try one of the many other beautiful beaches in San Diego.

SURF REPORT

Grandview beach is one of four main breaks in Leucadia. Kelp beds just offshore help keep this break glassy long after other San Diego breaks are blown out. Best at a low to medium tide, catch it on a west or northwest swell for a good session.

BEACH KEY

Enjoy these activities and amenities while visiting Grandview:

Lifeguards
Surfing
Bodyboarding
Telephone

49

Beacon's

Beach Access: *Located along Neptune Avenue in Encinitas. Take the I-5 freeway and exit Leucadia Blvd., west. Turn right onto Neptune Avenue. Turn left into Beacon's parking lot and walk down the steep, sandy hill to the beach.*
Beach Hours: *5:00am – 10:00pm*

For many of San Diego's North County surfers, Beacon's is much more than a beach with good waves. It is a second home, and the fellow surfers - members of their family. On any given day, the warm soulful sounds of crashing

waves call to the locals that lay claim to this beach. Fellows with names like Kahuna Bob, Sea Ghost, and Ricardo de Grande Aqua show up to check the waves and catch up with friends. If there is any kind of swell, they make their way down the steep, narrow footpath to the beach and take to the water like birds to flight, each with their own distinctive style. Between sets, locals initiate new guys into the family by bestowing nicknames according to their talents and personality: like Diva and Artist who got their names by painting murals on her surfboards, and Long Willy who pretends he's a shortboarder until it's time to surf and breaks out his long board.

As the sun sinks below the horizon signaling surfers that evening is approaching, they gradually and somewhat reluctantly yield to the day's end. They exit the water and then slowly dawdle backwards up the hill sporting smiles as radiant as the sun as they look back onto the beach and their eyes glass over with memories of the day.

Beacon's is probably the most recognized named break in Leucadia. This beach features two main peaks and like other Leucadia beaches remains glassy until mid-morning due to off-shore kelp beds. This beach is best on a low to medium tide and takes just about any swell direction.

DIVE REPORT

On days when the waves are flat and the wind is still, don mask and fins and head out to the kelp bed for an interesting dive where you may encounter anything from a Leopard Shark to a Shovelnose Guitarfish or California Halibut.

BEACH KEY

Enjoy these activities and amenities while visiting Beacon's:

Lifeguards
Surfing
Bodyboarding
Sunbathing
Fishing
Spear Fishing
Telephone

51

Stone Steps

Beach Access: *Located along South El Portal and Neptune Avenue in Encinitas. Take the I-5 freeway, exit Leucadia Blvd., west. Turn left onto N. Coast Hwy. Turn right on S. El Portal Street. Stay to the left and continue around the curve. Cross over Neptune Avenue. Park free along the residential streets. Walk down the long stairway to the beach.*
Beach Hours: *5:00am – 2:00am*

Many surfers share the dream of surfing at a secret beach, where the ride is clean and long and the waves belong solely to them. In Encinitas, a handful of locals and visitors who have ventured off the beaten path, have discovered Stone Steps to be such a place.

Possibly the most secret of all the beaches in Encinitas, Stone Steps is well worth the effort of discovery. Located at the end of a one-way street and hidden beneath towering sandstone bluffs, this beach is actually a narrow ribbon of strand too tiny for most on-shore activities, but ideal for surfing, bodyboarding, and surf-fishing.

Stone Steps features uncrowded, variable peaks where surfers can get a fun ride during low to medium tide on just about any swell.

Enjoy these activities and amenities while visiting Stone Steps:

Lifeguards
Surfing
Bodyboarding
Skimboarding
Surf Fishing

The Beaches of San Diego

Moonlight State Beach

Beach Access: *Located along Third and C Street in Encinitas. Take the I-5 freeway to Encinitas exit Encinitas Boulevard, west. Cross over Highway 101. Turn left onto Third Street. Turn right onto C Street. Turn right into the parking lot. Follow the gently sloping hill to the beach.* **Beach Hours:** *5:00am – 2:00am*

In the early 1920's, families would often saunter down the gently sloping hill of Encinitas Boulevard – toting baskets filled with cheese, wine and soda – to picnic on the sandy knoll at Moonlight State Beach. Once there, they would arrange their hors d'oeuvres and watch transfixed as the moon rose and illuminated the crashing waves, giving this beach its well-suited name: Moonlight State Beach. Today, little has changed. The charm and appeal of this small, seaside strand still lures families to picnic along its shores.

Moonlight State Beach

Only now, instead of aperitifs, they enjoy sandwiches and snow cones sold from the local snack stand.

Perhaps, the biggest draw for visitors is the variety of amenities offered at Moonlight, and the fact that this beach caters to both teens and toddlers. Adults can join in a game of volleyball, while teens take to the water to surf or dive. Children can dig for sand crabs, or play Peter Pan on a make-believe, Captain Hook pirate ship complete with decks, slides, periscopes and swings, then nap under the spreading shade of a thatched palapa.

At Moonlight State Beach surfing takes a back seat to playing on the sand. But for those who just want to get wet these average to intermediate beach breaks will do the job just fine.

Enjoy these activities and amenities while visiting Moonlight State Beach:

Lifeguards
Swimming
Surfing
Skimboarding
Bodyboarding
Bodysurfing
Scuba Diving
Spear Fishing
Volleyball
Playground
Fire Rings
Barbecues
Picnic Tables
Snack Bar
Restrooms
Showers

![Beach Key]
BEACH KEY

![Dive Report]
DIVE REPORT

Reef and kelp dive at Moonlight State Beach:

To reach the kelp site, enter just north of the beach volleyball courts and swim fifty yards offshore. Here, large kelp patties house species like Calico Bass, Barred Sand Bass, Giant Kelpfish and Thornback. On a good day divers see Halibut, Sheephead, and Leopard Sharks.

To reach the reef, enter between the two palms on the north side of the beach and swim thirty yards offshore. The reef will be about fifteen feet below, where exotic coraline algae, sea fans, and nudibranchs abound.

57

D Street Beach

Beach Access: *Traveling north or south along the I-5 freeway, exit Encinitas Boulevard, west. Turn left onto South Coast Highway 101. Turn right onto D Street. Park free along the residential streets and walk down the long stairway to the beach.* **Beach Hours:** *4:00am – 2:00am*

Just south of the crowds and clamor of Moonlight State Beach lies D Street, a small ribbon of sand framed by tall bluffs and populated by local high school and college age kids. Cute suntanned girls and surfer boys loll on the sand in small cliques waiting for surf. As one of Encinitas' stand out surf spots, D Street has great shape and consistent beach breaks. One local describes it, "like a skate park in the water, with barrels, bowls, rampy sections and steep walls."

When a big swell rolls in and D Street is closing out, surfers make their way a couple hundred yards south along the beach to Boneyards, accessible only via the stairway at D Street. Although it is a place perhaps best known for its surf, it also caters to a small population of beachgoers who come here to bathe a la natural. During low tide, Boneyard's tall cliffs and narrow shoreline, which is checkered with large boulders, afford nudists a small measure of privacy.

At high tide the ocean claims back both beaches, causing the shoreline to virtually disappear beneath the waves.

Test your surfing prowess on the variety of peaks, bowls, tubes, and rampy sections at D Street. Just make sure your at the top of you're game as this area is dominated by locals and experienced surfers. Best on a medium tide and southwest swell.

When the waves close out at D Street, head to Boneyards for long fun lefts or short steep rights. Check the waves from the K Street view point, before committing to the long walk from D Street.

Enjoy these activities and amenities while visiting D Street Beach:

Lifeguards
Surfing
Bodyboarding
Skimboarding
Bodysurfing
Surf Fishing
Showers
Clothing Optional
(Boneyards Only)

BEACH KEY

59

Swami's

Beach Access: *Traveling north or south along the I-5 freeway, exit Encinitas Boulevard, west. Turn left onto South Coast Highway 101. Turn right at Sea Cliff County Park. Park free in the lot or along the highway. Walk down a steep stairway to the beach.*
Beach Hours: *4:00am – 2:00am*

Driving along Historic Route 101, on approach to Encinitas, many a traveler's vision becomes captivated by the Self-Realization Fellowship Retreat - an enormous structure with lotus-shaped towers and flower filled gardens. The scene looks more like an illustration

from some marvelous book of Eastern fairy tales than something that belongs in a beach town. It's a view that most visitors don't expect to see along the coast, but just beyond its grounds lays one of the best surfing beaches in San Diego. Aptly named Swami's after the developer of the Self-Realization Fellowship Retreat, this beach is all about surfing.

In 1971, The Beach Boy's made this beach famous in their hit song "Surfin' U.S.A."; but long before that locals have known Swami's as one of the best spots to surf high-quality waves which break clean and hollow even on the biggest days when San Diego's other prime surfing spots become choppy and unridable. On any given day, anywhere from 50-150 surfers, intent on catching an epic ride, can be seen forming tight clusters in the lineup. This beach is for experienced surfers and has a loyal local following complete with their very own surfing association.

61

San Elijo State Beach

Beach Access: *Traveling along Highway 101 in Encinitas, turn west into the San Elijo State Beach parking lot, or park for free, along the Pacific Coast Highway directly across from the park. From the I-5 Freeway, exit Encinitas Blvd. Turn left on to the Pacific Coast Highway. Park in the San Elijo State Beach parking lot or free along the Pacific Coast Highway.* **Beach Hours:** *7:00am – 10:00pm*
Reservation Info: *(800) 444-7275*

Ditch the watch. Forward all calls. And as Bob Marley sings, "Don't worry 'bout a thing". For those who discover that their daily schedule is much too chaotic and find themselves wishing for a simpler life – perhaps one that revolves around the rise and fall of ocean tides - grab the tent, hammock, surfboard, and sunscreen and head to San Elijo State Beach and Campground for a carefree and fun-filled break.

At San Elijo State Beach, visitors have their choice of 171 bluff top campsites. Only about half of the campsites have ocean views, but all are within earshot of the crashing waves. Make certain to reserve your campsite at least seven months in advance, since the campground fills quickly, especially in the summer.

San Elijo State Beach is a place which transports its visitors to another time - where bicycles are the standard method of transportation and dinnertime means family and friends roasting hotdogs over an open fire.

And while the environment is mostly relaxing, the park itself can be quite exciting. During the day, visitors can take one of six stairways to the beach to surf, sunbathe, and explore the tidepools. Or, hike along coastal trails, walk along the lagoon preserve, and bird watch.

At night, the park features interpretive programs where campers have the opportunity to talk with park rangers around a campfire and learn about the marine environment and its animals, as well as watch a short clip about the history of surfing.

San Elijo State Beach's reef system produces scattered small peaks ideal for those learning to surf. However, there are four standout spots for more experienced surfers: Pipes, Tippers, Campgrounds & Suckouts.

Pipes and Tippers - the northern most breaks, next to Swami's, are consistent lefts which peels over a shallow slab of rock. During lower tides, the right is fast and steep.

Campgrounds – located directly in front of the campground store is a small peak that can get fast and hollow especially during a winter swell.

Suckouts – just 50 yards north of Cardiff State Beach, is an advanced break. This thick, dredging barrel crashes over a reef in very shallow water and closes out on anything above six feet.

Enjoy these activities and amenities while visiting San Elijo State Beach:

Lifeguards
Swimming
Surfing
Scuba Diving
Snorkeling
Surf Fishing
Birdwatching
Hiking Trails
Bike Trails
Tent Camping
R.V. Camping
Camp Store
Picnic Tables
Fire Rings
Parking Fee
Restrooms
Showers
Visitor Center
Dogs Permitted
(in campground only - not on beach)

Cardiff State Beach

Beach Access: *Traveling north or south along the I-5 freeway, exit Lomas Sante Fe Drive, west. Turn right onto the Pacific Coast Highway 101. Turn left to park in the lot at Seaside or continue one mile and turn left into the parking lot at Cardiff Reef.*
Beach Hours: *7:00am – Sunset*

Cardiff State Beach's 1.7 miles of coastline is divided into two separate areas: Cardiff Reef to the north and Seaside to the south. And while this strand is technically one beach, the atmosphere between the two areas is quite different: Cardiff Reef is filled with laidback surfing families, while Seaside attracts more of a younger surfing crowd and beachgoers interested in tidepooling.

At Cardiff Reef it's the locals who set this beach apart from any other beach in San Diego. Their carefree lifestyle and surf traditions create an atmosphere that is reminiscent of surfing's more innocent days of Gidget and Moondoggie.

Cardiff Reef &
Seaside Reef
are the two reef breaks
at Cardiff State Beach.
For longboarders, Cardiff
features slow and mushy
waves that make long
mellow noserides. Best at
low to medium tide on a
northwest or west swell.
During a winter swell,
the reef can get fast and
hollow. Seaside Reef is
a popular local surf spot.
When it's going off, it can
get downright crowded.
This reef is best at low
tide, when the waves
spit out barrels that break
over the shallow reef.

DIVE REPORT

When the surf
is calm and the
water clear,
Cardiff Reef,
Seaside Reef and
Tabletops may prove to
be one of the most exciting
dive areas in San Diego.
This designated under-
water park features
hollows, channels, kelp
patties and surf grass that
provide shelter for animals
such as sheep-crab, lobster,
sheephead, and banded
and shovel-nose guitarfish.
Also, archaeological data
suggests that there are
22 prehistoric sites, 1
known shipwreck and
3 sea vessels that are
reported to be lost here.

Cardiff State Beach

It's a place where locals gather in the parking lot, around the barbecue, and in the water to catch up with family and friends and invariably talk about surfing. In typical Cardiff fashion, days are spent greeting one another with a friendly smile and a quick nod of the head on the way out to the reef, where devoted surfers walk the nose, hang ten or just cruise down the face of blue-gray waves. When the surf is flat, beachgoers take to snorkeling or scuba diving the underwater park, or enjoy dining at the mexican or seafood restaurants that line the strand.

At Seaside, the cobblestone strand may seem a bit unappealing to most visitors, especially those looking to sunbathe, but just south of the strand lies a series of small sandy inlets and a reef dubbed Tabletops where beachgoers both young and old can idyll away the day poking about in tidepools, examining 45- million-year-old fossils embedded in the rocks, and counting the endless number of fish while snorkeling the reef.

BEACH KEY

Enjoy these activities and amenities while visiting Cardiff State Beach:

Lifeguards
Surfing
Kite Surfing
Swimming
Paddleboarding
Bodyboarding
Skimboarding
Kayaking
Scuba Diving
Snorkeling
Spear Fishing
Surf Fishing
Tidepools
Dogs Permittted
(on a leash)
Restaurants
(close by)

69

CHAPTER FOUR

Solana Beach

The Beaches of San Diego

Tide Park

Beach Access: *Traveling north or south along the I-5 freeway, exit Lomas Santa Fe Drive, west. Turn right onto the Pacific Coast Highway 101. Turn left onto Solana Vista Drive. Park free along the residential street at Solana Vista Drive and Pacific Avenue. Walk down the long wooden stairway to the beach.* **Beach Hours:** *7:00am – Sunset*

Visitors who come to Tide Park may feel a bit like a fish at the bottom of a fishbowl. This horseshoe-shaped cove has tall unstable bluffs with hundreds of houses and families perched atop, all peering down on the sunbathers. However, once visitors enter the water, the setting quickly becomes serene and Tide Park's wall of houses fades into a backdrop of tall cliffs, caramel colored sand and blue ocean.

The surfing here is good. Many Solana Beach locals wake at the break of dawn, and while the rest of the town slumbers, surf until their arms get tired. When the ocean goes flat, the cove becomes the domain of snorkelers, fishermen, swimmers, and at low tide, tide poolers.

This local classic spits out fast, hollow waves that break right over the reef. Catch it during a south or southwest swell at mid tide from 3–5 feet for a great session.

DIVE REPORT

Just north of the stairs, Tabletop Reef glistens in the sun. When the surf goes flat and the tide scrolls back, don a snorkel and mask and explore the scattered reefs and kelp beds directly offshore.

BEACH KEY

Enjoy these activities and amenities while visiting Tide Park:

Lifeguards
Surfing
Bodyboarding
Skimboarding
Snorkeling
Scuba Diving
Surf Fishing
Sunbathing
Tidepools
Showers

Fletcher Cove

Beach Access: *Traveling north or south along the I-5 freeway, exit Lomas Santa Fe Drive, west. Continue over the Pacific Coast Highway 101. Park in the lot and walk down a gently sloping paved walkway to the beach.*
Beach Hours: *6:00am – 10:00pm*

When the days become longer, and the sun becomes warmer and summer has finally arrived, many Solana Beach families find it is the perfect time of year to return to their favorite neighborhood beach: Fletcher Cove. Many locals arrive by bike using the two-mile-long paved bike path located just east of the 101, where there are benches that provide resting areas for families with small children. Those from out of town may choose to take the coaster that delivers its passengers just three short blocks from the strand. Or simply drive to the beach and park in the free public parking lot.

This little jewel of a place has a grassy park with a half basketball court and one picnic bench that overlooks twin crescent beaches and a spectacular stretch of San Diego. The coves are man made and were constructed years ago using hydraulic hoses and steam shovels to erode the cliffs. Today, everyone from junior lifeguards, surfers, swimmers, parents and kids enjoy this small slice of paradise and happily play along almost every inch of its waterfront in the summer months. Just two blocks away, bric-a-brac shops, hamburger stands, and sit-down restaurants abound and make a perfect complement to a day at the beach.

During summer, the beach is divid- ed into swimming and surfing areas. The surfing areas are located to the north and south of the two coves. Both breaks feature a typical beach break.

Enjoy these activities and amenities while visiting Fletcher Cove:

Lifeguards
Surfing
Swimming
Bodyboarding
Skimboarding
Basketball
Park
Picnic Tables
Showers
Restrooms
Restaurants (close by)
Shopping (close by)
Wheelchair Accessible

75

Seascape Surf

Beach Access: *Located along South Sierra Ave. and North Seascape Surf in Solana Beach. Traveling north or south on the I-5 freeway, exit Via De La Valle, west. Turn right onto S. Sierra Ave. and park free along the street at N. Seascape Surf. Walk down a narrow alley and steep stairway to the beach.*
Beach Hours: *6:00am – 10:00pm*

Seascape Surf: The name itself conjures up images of a picturesque strand, with azure blue waves crashing onto a sun kissed beach. An apt description, especially when visited during low tide at day's end.

During sunset, this beach is one of the loveliest in San Diego. As the sun sinks into the Pacific, its rays bounce off the bluffs making everything instantly warm and colorful. The sheer cliffs become a riot of yellow and gold, and the sea turns a deep and vivid blue.

Perhaps the best way to experience this beach is to stroll along its strand at dusk, and once the sun arrives at its finale, make your way up the stairway and across the street to the Beach Walk where you can enjoy shopping or a meal at one of the many restaurants.

During the summer months surfing is restricted to the area designated by the black and white checked flags. Here, surfers will find a typical beach break with shifting peaks.

Enjoy these activities and amenities while visiting Seascape Surf:

Lifeguards
Surfing
Swimming
Bodyboarding
Skimboarding
Surf Fishing
Beachcombing
Showers
Restaurants (close by)
Shopping (close by)

Del Mar Shores

Beach Access: *Traveling north or south along the I-5 freeway, exit Via De La Valle, west. Turn right onto Sierra Avenue and park free in one of two lots. Walk down Sierra Avenue just past Via de la Valle and walk down the alleyway and stairway to the beach.*
Beach Hours: *6:00am – 10:00pm*

The access to Del Mar Shores may give the term "long haul" new meaning. The approach requires a lengthy walk through an alley followed by five long flights of near-vertical stairs. But once visitors reach this sunny cove and plunge into the surf, they will find it well worth the effort.

Each summer, this beach fills with Solana Beach locals and out-of-towners who are staying at the timeshare condos located high on the cliffs above. These vacationers settle in quickly and make this beach their own. Every day they set up large blue canopies and the whole community turns out to sun along the strand, swim in the ocean, scoop up clams by the handful and catch up with friends after a long winter apart.

The timeshare residents aren't the only ones fond of Del Mar Shores. Along the north end of the cove and about 100 yards offshore lives a seal. Its dark bald head can be seen bobbing above the water and when a pod of dolphins pass, this territorial seal can be heard barking out warnings to steer clear of his domain. As one Solana Beach local puts it, "Del Mar Shores is such a nice beach that even the seal wants it all to himself".

The difficult beach access may impede many surfers to ride this break, but for the dedicated surfer who doesn't mind carrying a board five flights of stairs, you will find a nice, uncrowded beach break at the north end of the cove.

Enjoy these activities and amenities while visiting Del Mar Shores:

Lifeguards
Surfing
Swimming
Bodysurfing
Bodyboarding
Skimboarding
Sunbathing
Showers

CHAPTER FIVE

Del Mar

Del Mar City Beach

Beach Access: *Traveling along the I-5 freeway, exit Via De La Valle west. Continue straight to the Pacific Coast Highway. To reach North Beach, park along the highway at Via De La Valle, and walk down the dirt hill to the beach. To reach North 15th Street Beaches, park along the Pacific Coast Highway or any of the residential streets and walk to the beach. To reach South 15th Street Beaches, continue along the Pacific Coast Highway to the intersection of 15th street and turn west. Park along the street and walk through Seagrove Park to the beach, or continue further south and take one of the dirt trails down from the cliffs.* **Beach Hours:** *24 hours*

Tourists and residents of Del Mar have been known to boast of endless summer days spent riding roller coasters at the fair, late afternoons jumping the waves at the beach and summer evenings betting on horses at the track. In late summer though, when the fair and track have closed their doors, tourists and residents find that the best way to fill their days is with sun, sand and surf at Del Mar City Beach.

If beachgoers were to stroll the full length of the shoreline, they would find three distinct beaches: North Beach, North 15th Street Beaches, and South 15th Street Beaches. All feature a different ambiance, rules, and activities.

North Beach, located at Via Del La Valle and the Pacific Coast Highway, is widely held to be San Diego's number one dog beach. It's a place where dog- lovers come to play with their pets. And the dogs seem just as eager to cultivate the friendship. Small, medium and large sized animals: it makes no difference here, together they run, bark, roll-over, shake, fetch, and playfully push each other about, awed and delighted by the freedom of it all. Dogs are allowed off -leash September 15 through June 15.

There is more to North Beach than just dogs. For the past twenty-five years, San Diego businesses collectively sponsor an annual bocce ball tournament to benefit the Boys and Girls Club. More than 500 competitors vie for the title of Bocce Ball Champion, and over 1500 spectators come to cheer on their favorite team and enjoy the music and food from various San Diego restaurants.

Del Mar City Beach

North 15th Street Beaches extend between the San Dieguito river mouth (located at the south end of North Beach) and 15th Street. This long, wide stretch of beach, backed by waterside villas, painted in lyrical pastel colors, with sunny patios and masterful gardens, serves an ideal setting for a beach luau. Here, kids dance the limbo, race in relays and play volleyball, while parents socialize and barbecue burgers and hot dogs over the grill. To reach North 15th Street Beaches take any of the numbered streets west until you reach the sand.

As equally as marvelous a setting, South 15th Street Beaches encompass the stretch of sand between 15th Street and 4th Street. Perhaps the best way to experience this section of beach is to begin at bluff top Seagrove Park where rolling green lawns, dotted with park benches, sunbathers, picnickers and artists at their easels, spill over onto a well-populated golden strand. The park itself offers its visitors almost all the pleasures of the beach with the benefit of never having to get their feet sandy. But for those who prefer a little sand between their toes, take the winding path past the playground to the beach where there are volleyball courts, a good reef break, and a restaurant directly adjacent to the strand. Walk just 200 yards south and the crowds begin to thin and only a handful of runners and joggers dot the beach.

Probably the best, but also the most crowded spot along Del Mar City Beach, is the reef break at 15th Street. This wave is good for both long and short boarders. The left tends to be fast and long allowing for multiple turns down the line. The right tends to back off and get mushy. There are numerous other beach breaks along Del Mar City Beach. North of 15th Street surfers will find well-shaped top-to-bottom peaks. South of 15th Street 11th, 7th and 4th Street offer up some good waves.

Enjoy these activities and amenities while visiting Del Mar City Beach:

BEACH KEY

Lifeguards
Surfing
Swimming
Bodyboarding

Skimboarding	*Playground*
Kayaking	*Picnic Tables*
Snorkeling	*Barbecues*
Scuba Diving	*Fire Rings*
Fishing	*Restaurants*
Biking	*Restrooms*
Roller Blading	*Showers*
Park	*Rentals*

Torrey Pines State Beach

Beach Access: *Traveling south along the I-5 freeway, exit Del Mar Heights Road, west. Turn left onto Camino Del Mar. Turn right into the Torrey Pines parking lot at North Torrey Pines Road.*
Beach Hours: *8:00am – Sunset*
Torrey Pines Lodge Interperative Center: *(858) 755-8219*

Torrey Pines State Beach unfolds as a sweeping expanse of pine forest surrounded by the blue waters of the Pacific Ocean. Torrey Pines is unlike any other beach in San Diego, or for that matter in the world. Its uniqueness is defined by its 2,000-acre coastal hilltop wilderness where one of the world's most rare trees, the Torrey Pine, resides.

Torrey Pines State Beach has an interesting history, one that dates back thousands of years. The trees and environs are believed to be remnants of an ancient woodland that once thrived along the whole of Southern California's coast, but due to dramatic changes in the climate and landscape, the Torrey Pines died off everywhere, except this small stretch of Coastline in Del Mar, California and on Santa Rosa Island. As early as 1883, people recognized the Torrey Pines' beauty and value and helped establish safeguards in an effort to protect their delicate environment, going as far as offering a $100.00 reward in 1889 "for the detection and conviction of any person guilty of removing, cutting or otherwise destroying any of the Torrey Pines." Thanks in large part to their efforts, visitors today come from far and wide to witness the trees in their natural splendor.

Torrey Pines State Beach

There are so many lovely vistas and pleasurable activities here that it is nearly impossible to manage it all in one day. But a good place to begin is at the 1923 historic adobe lodge located high on the hill on North Torrey Pines Road. Once a way station for visitors traveling from Los Angles to San Diego, today this Southwest-styled structure serves as a visitors' center and museum and offers an introduction into the local history, animal-life, plants, and geology of the area

through various exhibits and tours. Enjoy a stroll through the native plant garden or wander out onto the lanai and take in the glorious views of the Los Peñasquitos Lagoon.

Quite possibly the best way to experience Torrey Pines State Beach and its 30,000 plus species of plants, animals, birds, and spiders is by hiking one of eleven marked nature trails. The paths wind their way through various terrains: harsh, windswept landscapes of red clay, on which the Torrey Pine trees seem like intrusions; brush-covered slopes, brightened in the spring by wildflowers; the lagoon, wreathed by brilliant green carpets of pickleweed. All are endearing in their natural beauty and have inspired writers, photographers, and artists for generations. Along the way, stop at the benches and viewpoints to be rewarded with a view of coastal splendor. For as far as the gaze can reach stretches a sunny, golden beach, and pelicans scudding an inch or so above the crystal blue water. Or better yet, take one of the hilltop trails down to the beach to enjoy the 4.7 mile-long strand. Docent led hikes are available year-round on weekends from 10:00 a.m. – 2:00 p.m.

SURF REPORT

Torrey Pines features a typical beach break. Variable peeks throughout the park spread out the crowds, so find your perfect break and paddle out for a fun ride.

BEACH KEY

Enjoy these activities and amenities while visiting Torrey Pines State Beach:

Lifeguards
Swimming
Surfing
Skimboarding
Bodyboarding
Surf Fishing
Bird Watching
Tide Pools
Hike Trails
Picnic Tables
Restrooms
Showers
Visitor Center
Beach Wheelchairs
Bus Stop
Parking Fee

CHAPTER SIX

La Jolla

Black's

Beach Access: *Traveling north or south along the I-5 Freeway, exit Genesee Avenue west. Turn left onto North Torrey Pines Road. Turn right onto La Jolla Shores Drive. Turn right onto La Jolla Farms Road. Park free along the residential street and walk through the gate, located at La Jolla Farms Road and Blackgold Road, down a long, paved and very steep road to the beach.* **Beach Hours:** *24 hours*

The combination of extreme surf, strong winds and sublime solitude draws a unique mix of people to Black's Beach. On any given day, you can meet a college student-turned professional surfer, a hang-glider and at least two nudists sprawled out on the beautiful two-mile crescent of beach. This cultural oddity creates a strand that is divided into north and south sections, each having completely different sensibilities.

The south end is where the "iron-men" of surfers ride fast moving giants. They have a passion for surfing, one that goes far beyond their fear of pain. When a winter swell stacks up waves that are triple overhead, they eagerly charge down the hill and enthusiastically paddle out, keen to feel the rush of ocean beneath their boards. They are in search of the perfect wave and ultimate ride. And with three peaks, including one whose break is sometimes as long as 200 yards, it's easily found.

Black's

At the north end of the beach, look up to witness the "Evil Kinevils" of hang-gliding and parasailing as they hurl themselves off the 300 foot cliffs – whizzing, flying, zooming, floating and defying gravity by sailing on warm updrafts that caress the headlands. It's a spectacular sight, a veritable rainbow of color: navy, yellow, red, orange, and white against a China blue sky and golden cliffs.

Below the cliffs, a yellow flag waves, signaling sun worshippers to the area where clothes and swimsuits are optional. Here, anyone bathing 'a la natural' is befriended by the 'tribes' and engaged in building sand castles, playing volleyball or throwing horseshoes. The relationships are colorful, complicated and always a bit of a mystery to the non-nudists. But at Black's beach all are accepted.

* Black's beach officially prohibits nudity, but since the area has such a long history of naturism it is often overlooked.

With year-round surf and notoriously big winter swells, Black's is considered by many to be the best beach break in San Diego. Just offshore lies a deepwater canyon that generates thick barreling waves that hold their shape during a large swell. Three main peaks give expert surfers a variety of rides. From a short, steep bowling right at North Peak, to a right or left at Middle Peak, to a long peeling left at South Peak. The waves are best at low tide on a northwest, west, or southwest swell.

Enjoy these activities and amenities while visiting Black's:

Lifeguards
Swimming
Surfing
Bodysurfing
Bodyboarding
Skimboarding
Volleyball
Hang Gliding
Dogs Permitted
Clothing Optional

BEACH KEY

La Jolla Shores

Beach Access: *Traveling south along the I-5 freeway, exit La Jolla Village Drive, west. Turn left onto Torrey Pines Road. Turn right onto Avenida de la Playa. Turn right onto Camino del Oro.*

Traveling north along the I-5 freeway, exit La Jolla Parkway. Stay on La Jolla Parkway for about two miles as it turns into Torrey Pines Road. Turn right onto Calle de la Plata. Turn left onto Avenida de la Playa. Turn right onto Camino del Oro. Park free along the street or follow Camino del Oro two blocks and park free in the lot. **Beach Hours:** *24 hours*

The California Coast is dotted with intimate coves which cater to scuba divers and snorkelers, expansive strands where surfers and swimmers delight in wave riding, and easily accessible beaches that furnish families with playground equipment, boardwalks, and enough sand to build castles as large as a child's imagination. But, if there's one beach in California that seems to have it all – scuba diving, snorkeling, kayaking, fishing, surfing, swimming, picnicing, shopping, biking, sunbathing, whale watching, tide pooling and even diving with sharks, it would have to be La Jolla Shores.

Million-dollar houses, resorts, and hotels – artfully jumbled together – make up the backdrop to beautiful Kellogg

Park and La Jolla Shores. Along its length, stretches a line of tall palms that unfolds onto an ocean-themed playground and beachside promenade where children race candy apple red bikes and scooters.

In the summer, a crowd fills every inch of waterfront. Surf camps and scuba diving classes congregate in the water. Umbrellas and beach chairs blanket the sand, and visitors lose themselves in a multiplicity of lively pursuits.

At the end of Avenida de la Playa, kayakers can drive their cars directly onto the shore to launch their crafts into the surf. Just 30 yards offshore, in water 5-10 feet deep, is the best place to drop in with a mask and snorkel and soar over schools of leopard sharks. Once topside, stroke just another 170 yards to a submarine canyon where in the winter fortunate kayakers can paddle alongside migrating California Grey whales, plus have a chance to see other marine mammals such as dolphins, seals, and sea lions.

For those visitors who enjoy less-thrilling pursuits, stretch out on a beach towel and fall asleep to the sound of guitar music as it is carried on the breeze from somewhere in the park. After a while, walk just two short blocks to Avenida de la Playa, where burger stands, pizza parlors, ice cream shops and sit-down restaurants are available. And if, after all this relaxation, the notion strikes that maybe a surf lesson or kayak excursion is in order, stop by La Jolla Kayak for them to arrange all the details.

A surfer-friendly vibe & good waves makes La Jolla Shores a favorite long and short-boarding spot. Scripp's Pier and La Jolla Shores both break best fall and winter on a west, or northwest swell. Summer, it's a great place to learn to surf. Join tourists, neophytes and surf students as they catch the froth, and whoop at the excitement of catching a wave.

There is nothing more enticing to divers than good visibility, deep-water canyons, interesting walls and a variety of ocean-dwelling species. Combine that with convenient parking, easy access and beach entry; paradise is found. To dive here, park at the foot of Vallecito Street. Gear up, wade past the breakers to the buoy to see schools of tiny rockfish, California arminas, San Diego dorids, gobies and much more.

DIVE REPORT

Enjoy these activities and amenities while visiting La Jolla Shores:

Lifeguards
Surfing
Swimming
Bodyboarding
Skimboarding   *Playground*
Kayaking   *Picnic Tables*
Snorkeling   *Barbecues*
Scuba Diving   *Fire Ring*
Fishing   *Restaurants*
Biking   *Restrooms*
Roller Blading   *Showers*
Park   *Rentals*

BEACH KEY

99

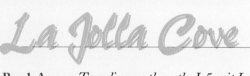

La Jolla Cove

Beach Access: *Traveling south on the I-5 exit La Jolla Village Drive, west. Turn left on Torrey Pines Road. Turn right onto Prospect Street. Turn right onto Coast Boulevard. Park along the street and walk down one of two stairways that lead to the beach.*

Traveling north on the I-5 exit La Jolla Parkway. La Jolla Parkway becomes Torrey Pines Road. Continue to Prospect Street, turn right. Turn right onto Coast Boulevard. Park along the street. Walk down one of two stairways that lead to the beach. **Beach Hours:** *24 hours*

I t's been said that, "Paradise is a necessary invention of the human mind." Indeed, it is a place where everything is beautiful and carefree, and for many, a place that they escape to regularly in their dreams. It's easy to spot, their eyes glass over, a contented look washes round their face, and they have arrived: Paradise found!

But for a select few San Diegans and even fewer vacationers, there is no need for imagination. They have discovered paradise right here at La Jolla Cove. Sitting on the viewpoint benches looking out over the small cusp of beach wrapped by golden bluffs and studded with palms, scuba divers, kayakers, open ocean swimmers, and visitors feel as though they are sitting on the prow of their very own beach paradise.

La Jolla Cove

Looking out towards the horizon, California brown pelicans soar inches above the water and black cormorants congregate on the white rock ledges. In the water, not more than 20 feet from the shore, bright orange Garibaldi, leopard sharks, rays, and various other fish flit between the green sea grass and kelp beds. Scuba divers, snorkelers, and kayakers take to the water to explore the underwater canyon and

seven sea caves. As the La Jolla Cove Swimmers Club ply through the waves, their colorful bathing caps bounce off the blue water.

At high tide, the beach virtually disappears. This is an excellent time to enjoy Scripp's Memorial Park, located directly above the beach. Its beautifully manicured green lawns and board-walk stretch 2.3 miles from La Jolla Cove to Wipeout beach. Businessmen in suits, moms with strollers, beachgoers, athletes, and vacationers from abroad all zip along the blufftop path taking in the fresh air and unobstructed views. Beyond the beach lies glitzy La Jolla Village where visitors can join the well-heeled residents and tourists in shopping and dining.

When other dive sites in San Diego are murky and have poor visibility, head to La Jolla Cove, whose bay is sheltered from the southerly swells that effect the rest of the La Jolla coastline. Visibility often reaches anywhere between 15 and 30 feet. A series of rock ledges, reefs, sand channels and sea caves gives divers the chance of seeing a variety of marine species including Moray eels, lobster, rockfish, garibaldi, angel sharks, halibut and seals. As part of the San Diego-La Jolla Underwater Ecological Reserve, this area is protected and divers may not remove or disturb the marine life. La Jolla Cove is a favorite dive destination for many scuba divers and snorkelers. As a result, it gets very crowded during the summer and on weekends. To avoid the crowds dive early in the morning or on weekdays.

Enjoy these activities and amenities while visiting La Jolla Cove:

Lifeguards
Swimming
Snorkeling
Scuba Diving
Kayaking
Rentals (close by)
Tide Pools
Park
Picnic Tables
Barbecues
Shopping
Restaurants
Showers
Restrooms

BEACH KEY

Children's Pool

Beach Access: *Traveling north or south along the I-5 freeway, exit La Jolla Villa Drive, west. Turn left onto Torrey Pines Road. Turn right onto Prospect Place. Turn right onto Coast Boulevard South. Turn right to stay on Coast Boulevard. Park free along Coast Boulevard and Jenner Street*
Beach Hours: *24 hours*

There they lie at the waterline, smashed together like sardines in a can on the small, tucked away inlet called Children's Pool. For the most part, they behave, content to lounge in the sun or play at the water's edge, but once in a while they bellow at one another and fence with their snouts in a no holds bar, out and out rustling match. These aren't children like the name would suggest, but rather large, furry gray sea lions and wild harbor seals.

Prior to 1931, Children's Pool was a coastal bluff called, "Seal Rock Point". In 1931, a sea wall was built connecting the coastal bluff to "Seal Rock", virtually closing off the channel and creating a salt-water pool where children could safely play. Over the years, the currents and gentle waves pushed sand into the cove and formed the beach today.

Now, when children come to Children's Pool, instead of splashing in the water, they ogle at the seals and sea lions that slide through the waves and flop onto the beach, seemingly unaware or indifferent to their presence. Volunteer naturalists from *La Jolla Friends of the Seals* stand ready to answer questions and are eager to share their love for the seals with anyone who is within earshot. Unfortunately, the City of La Jolla is hoping to dredge the beach and fashion it into a children's bathing pool again, effectively running off all the seals and sea lions.

While the future of Children's Pool is uncertain, visitors can be sure of one thing: Nothing is more heartwarming than an encounter with these special mammals in their own natural setting.

105

Wipeout

Beach Access: *Traveling north or south along the 1-5 freeway, exit La Jolla Village Drive, west. Turn left onto Torrey Pine Road. Turn right onto Prospect Place. Turn right onto Coast Boulevard South. Turn right to stay on Coast Boulevard. Park free along Coast Boulevard between Jenner Street and Coast Boulevard South.* **Beach Hours:** *24 hours*

Wipeout, the name resounds with each crashing wave. This aptly named, small cusp of beach, wrapped by low-lying cliffs, is perhaps best known for its steep beach and pulverizing shore break. Often compared to Newport Beach's, The Wedge and Oahu's, Sandy's Beach, Wipeout is a place where thrill seeking skimboarders and bodysurfers find their next dose of adrenaline.

It's nearly as exciting to watch, as it is to participate. On the shore, skimboarders jostle for position. As the wave is just about to break, they throw down their boards, skim into the water, then soar into the air, momentarily suspended, until they flip and slap sideways against the sea.

Meanwhile, in the water, bodysurfers vie for position in the waves. As the set hits, some take off dolphin style kicking both fins together, others backstroke into the wave then roll sideways as they navigate through the rushing tubes only to be deposited onto the shore in a few inches of water.

Hospital's

Beach Access: *Traveling north or south along the I-5 freeway, exit La Jolla Villa Drive, west. Turn left onto Torrey Pines Road. Turn right onto Prospect Place. Turn right onto Coast Boulevard South. Turn right to stay on Coast Boulevard. Park free along Coast Boulevard, between Culver Street and Coast Boulevard South.* **Beach Hours:** *24 hours*

The sweet smoky scent of summertime barbeque wafts across the grassy knoll just above Hospital's Point. This small stretch of lawn overlooks a thin sliver of sand that is threaded with rocky outcrops and reefs and is more suited for walking or poking around tidepools than for swimming. Popular with locals and tourists, visitors find families sitting around tables adorned with red checkered cloths, idling away the day picnicking, reading and in the evening-watching the setting sun.

At low tide, the ocean draws back to reveal a series of rock benches studded with limpets that sparkle like jewels under the mid-day sun. Explore around these crocodile shaped reefs at low tide. Or at high tide, don a snorkel, mask and fins and soar through the shallows to see a myriad of fish, anemones, sea stars, and an underwater rock arch.

For visitors who prefer to walk on water rather than swim through it, grab a board and surf the point. This uncrowded spot takes a little luck and a lot of expertise, but hollow tubes and steep lefts make it a regional classic.

This advanced reef break works best on a west or north west swell. Get tubed on the take off then speed down the steep face. Many surfers surf this break before attempting the more difficult and crowded neighboring Horseshoe reef.

When the waves are flat and the tide is up, Hospital Point makes a great shallow, reef dive. Roughly 300 yards from shore the bottom gently drops to a depth of 40 feet and gives way to reefs and sand channels. Look for octopi, lobsters, bat rays, halibut, and game fish among the reef.

Enjoy these activities and amenities while visiting Hospital's:

Surfing
Bodyboarding
Scuba Diving
Snorkeling
Surf Fishing
Picnic Area
Tide Pools

Marine Street

Beach Access: *Located at the foot of Marine Street in La Jolla. Traveling along the I-5 freeway south, exit Genessee Avenue west. Turn left onto Torrey Pines Road. Turn left onto Girard Avenue. Turn right onto Pearl Street. Turn left onto La Jolla Boulevard and then right onto Marine Street. Park free along the residential streets and make your way down to the beach.*

Traveling along the I-5 freeway north exit Torrey Pines Road. Turn left on Girard Avenue. Turn right on Pearl Street. Turn left onto La Jolla Boulevard and then right onto Marine Street. Park free along the residential streets and make your way down to the beach. **Beach Hours:** *24 hours*

Marine Street is La Jolla locals' favorite beach. Each summer throngs of neighborhood families, high school kids, and club water polo and La Crosse teams share Marine Street's white sandy shore. This playing and partying mix of people believe when it comes to the beach - the more the merrier.

The hub of social life is in the ocean. Marine Street's steep, fast and hollow shore break is ideal for skim boarding

and bodysurfing. With each set, bodysurfing bravados jockey for position, then hurl themselves through the thick tube of rushing water - the ocean beneath their belly and a mountain of water over their head. Sometimes, three or four bodies whiz past in a blur of whitewash on a "party wave". For them it is a quick fix of adrenaline; but for the bystanders on shore, it's a thrilling waterman show.

The beach itself is a long and lovely crescent framed on either end by rocky outcrops which serve as a great break for surfers and as a playground for children at low tide. Wide eyed kids splash through the shallow pools trying to catch the little tide pool fish or float on their backs simply taking in all the sights of summer.

Marine Street features two surf breaks: Horseshoe (north) and Little Point (south). Little Point, a left breaking wave, is a favorite point break among goofy footed surfers. Rarely crowded, and fairly consistent, all that is needed is careful timing and understanding the wave breaks. A few quick paddles, jump up on the board and glide effortlessly down the line. Breaks best during a south swell.

BEACH KEY

Activities and amenities while visiting Marine Street:

Lifeguards
Surfing
Swimming
Bodysurfing
Skimboarding
Bodyboarding
Snorkeling
Fishing
Tide Pools
Volleyball
Dogs Permitted
(on leash 6 pm – 9 am)

Windansea

Beach Access: *Located along Neptune Place in La Jolla. Traveling along the I-5 south exit La Jolla Village Drive, right. Turn left onto Torrey Pines Road. Left onto Girard Avenue. Right onto Pearl Street. Left onto La Jolla Boulevard. Right onto Nautilus Street. Then left onto Neptune Place.*

Traveling along the I-5 north, exit Ardath Road. Ardath Road becomes Torrey Pines Road. Turn left onto Girard Ave. Turn right onto Pearl Street. Left onto La Jolla Boulevard. Right onto Nautilus Street. Then left onto Neptune Place. Park along the residential streets or in the small parking lot and walk to the beach. **Beach Hours:** *24 hours*

Walking along the sandy shore at Windansea, the footprints of past surfing legends mingle with today's surfing greats. Long before surfing grabbed a hold of California's heart, a handful of San Diego locals discovered Windansea's consistent rolling waves. It was in the early 1940's when these 'first generation' surfers fell in love with the sport. For them, surfing was a way of life, a state of freedom and individual expression with its own rules, customs and amusements. Think *Endless Summer*, beach luaus, bonfires, and romantic encounters on the sand. Their way of life gave rise to today's modern beach culture. In 1946, they built the distinctive palm frond shack that looks out over the main reef break. Now a historic landmark, the shack, more fondly known as the 'Sugar Shack' - for the countless couples who exchanged sweet passions beneath its fronds- stands as a shrine to their bohemian roots.

In the 1960's, Windansea was home to surf legends like Pat Curren, Joey Cabell, Mike Hynson, Skip Frye and Billy Castor. They too fell into the soulful rhythm of the beach and lived a classic surf culture life. In 1968, they became the inspiration for Tom Wolfe's *The Pump House Gang*.

This beach continues to host famous surfers. On summer days, beachgoers can look out over the crowded shore and see couples playing smash ball or the unwary tourist being tossed about in the surf. But come fall, the locals reclaim the beach and the waves and carry on the long standing tradition of living for the surf.

113

South Windansea

Beach Access: *Traveling south along the I-5 freeway exit La Jolla Village Drive, west. Turn left onto Torrey Pines Road. Turn left onto Girard Avenue. Turn right onto Pearl Street. Turn left onto La Jolla Boulevard. Turn right onto Palomar Avenue.*

Traveling north along the I-8 freeway, exit West Mission Bay Drive, northwest. Bear right onto the ramp. Continue west onto West Mission Bay Drive. Turn right onto Mission Boulevard. Turn left onto La Jolla Boulevard. Turn left onto Palomar Avenue. Park free along the residential streets and take a short wooden stairway to the beach. **Beach Hours:** *24 hours*

A white-washed wooden stairway, discreetly hidden among seaside castles, gives way to one of the loveliest beaches in San Diego: South Windansea. This beach is equally as serene and picturesque as any tropical paradise.

When the sea is calm, visitors will find a Technicolor blue lagoon that washes over a sun-kissed shore checkered with tide pools, rock benches, and walls that create private inlets to block the wind and serve as shelters for romantics. Initials and names carved into the moss covered rock benches tell of lovers who once visited.

At low tide, the ocean rolls back unbroken to reveal a reef teeming with sea life so vivid beachgoers may feel as though they have stumbled into their own private aquarium. Beneath the flowing waves of green sea grass and kelp lay ochre sea stars, spiny purple urchins and sea anemones in lipstick pink and sea foam green.

Conversely, when the tide is high and the waves are pumping, South Windansea transforms into a surfer's paradise. Hollow barrels ripping off the side of Big Rock give experienced board riders some of their best rides.

South Windansea's surf break, Big Rock, is one of those places that you have to be a little out of your mind or really confident in your surfing abilities to surf. This heavy, left break- ing wave can churn out epic barrels, but it breaks over a shallow reef, so even a small mistake can end in an injury. Catch it during a mid to high tide on a west swell. Experienced surfers only!

BEACH KEY

Enjoy these activities and amenities while visiting South Windansea:

Surfing
Swimming
Bodyboarding
Snorkeling
Tide Pools
Kayaking
Surf Fishing
Spear Fishing

115

CHAPTER SEVEN

Pacific Beach

Tourmaline Surf Park

Beach Access: *Traveling along the I-5 freeway north or south, exit Garnet Avenue, west. Merge onto Mission Bay Drive. Turn left onto Grand Avenue. Turn right onto Mission Boulevard. Turn left onto La Jolla Boulevard. Turn left onto Tourmaline Street and park free in the public parking lot.*
Beach Hours: *24 hours*

Once in a while there is a beach that stands out against all the others. One that, for no apparent reason, holds the heart. A beach that upon arrival immediately feels like home and, like a distant love, you long for when apart. Tourmaline Surf Park is one such beach for a gang of locals who hang onto the vanishing lifestyle of the classic California beach culture of the 1960's and 70's.

Every morning, when dawn is pink and the streetlights are still on, Volkswagen buses, pickup trucks, vans, and cars with surf racks all cruise into the parking lot at Tourmaline Park. This is when the ocean is at its calmest and the waves call to surfers, old and young alike, to ride the smooth form-

ing peaks. The surfers reply by dropping their board into the water and paddling out to catch the next big set. For them, surfing here in the early morning is more than a daily ritual, it is more like a daily necessity. As one local puts it, "A few hours in the water and the rest of the day, no matter what happens, is enchanted."

It's more than just the surf that makes these locals feel at home, it's the camaraderie and warm hospitality. The hub of the social scene is in the parking lot. Surfers sit on the back of their tailgates and swap surf stories over a cup of coffee or around the hibachi. It's their version of the "aloha barbecue". Everyone is welcome. A glass interpretive case holds recent articles about the beach's surfing and fishing, as well as a tide chart. Mustard, catsup, relish, hot sauce and an onion are placed on top of the frame, in case someone forgot theirs.

Tourmaline Surf Park features two named breaks: The Point and Old Man's, which also is referred to Tourmaline Canyon. The Point is primarily a right that breaks over a rocky reef. It takes a good-sized west swell to wake this sleeping giant, but when it's on, its steep drops and quick bottom turns make it well worth the wait.

Old Man's, located at the north end of the beach, is a slow peeling wave that breaks both right and left. It's a great break for long boarders and beginning surfers.

Activities and amenities while visiting Tourmaline Surf Park:

Lifeguards
Surfing
Tide Pools
Park
Picnic Tables
Restrooms
Showers

BEACH KEY

Pacific Beach

Beach Access: *Traveling north or south along the I-5 freeway, exit Garnet Avenue/ Balboa Avenue, west. Merge onto Mission Bay Drive. Turn left onto Grand Avenue. Turn right onto Mission Boulevard. Turn left onto Garnet Avenue. Park along Ocean Boulevard, from Thomas Avenue to Diamond Street and walk to the beach.*
Beach Hours: *9:00 a.m. - 6:00 p.m.*

There's a parade in progress nearly everyday at Pacific Beach. A mish-mash of party-goers, bicyclists, street performers, college students, dancing in-line skaters, dog-walkers, joggers, and homeless vagabonds with their scribbled on cardboard signs, fill every inch of the over two mile long beachside boardwalk.

Pacific Beach

The scene is somewhat reminiscent of LA's Venice Beach with its muscular, tattooed men and scantily clothed women. A variety of unique shops along the boardwalk offers everything from body piercing and tattoos to ice cream and beach equipment rentals. It's all here and it all provides beachgoers with a chance to break free from the norm and experience life P.B. style.

Possibly the most quintessential P.B. experience is to join the throngs of people along Ocean Front Walk and allow yourself to become swept up in its festive carnival spirit. Along the way, tuck into one of the local shoreline watering holes where fat, warm tones resonate from outdoor speakers and ice-cold beer flows like water from the tap. Eventually, as the mood and music spill back out onto the boardwalk, and marathon revelers strut their stuff, challenge one to a game of horseshoes or volleyball.

When the shoulder-to-shoulder crowds become a little too thick and something roomier sounds oh-so sweet, then steal away to the historic Crystal Pier or smooth out a blanket just north of the pier where the crowds are thinner and the vibe is more laid back.

A well-shaped sandbar peak adjacent to Crystal Pier affords intermediate surfers with a long, fast left. Of course, like every-thing else in Pacific Beach, the wave becomes crowded during the summer. The best bet is to find an uncrowded, established sandbar break along the over two-mile strand. During the summer months, a designated surfing-only zone extends from Crystal Pier to Diamond Street. Diamond Street to Law Street is reserved for swimming only.

Enjoy these activities and amenities while visiting Pacific Beach:

Lifeguards
Surfing
Swimming
Bodyboarding
Skimboarding
Volleyball
Fishing
Fishing Pier
Biking
Roller Blading
Rentals
Shopping
Restaurants
Showers
Restrooms
Parking Fee

BEACH KEY

123

CHAPTER EIGHT

Mission Beach

Mission Beach

Beach Access: *Traveling south along the I-5 freeway, exit Sea World Drive, right. Take the ramp onto West Mission Bay Drive. Exit onto West Mission Bay Drive. Turn left onto Mission Boulevard and park free in the lot.*

Traveling north along the I-5 freeway, merge onto I-8 West toward Beaches. Take the West Mission Bay Drive exit towards Sports Arena Boulevard. Turn right onto West Mission Bay Drive. Exit onto West Mission Bay Drive. Turn left onto Mission Boulevard and park free in the lot
Beach Hours: *4:00am – 2:00am*

Riding the historic wooden roller coaster - as it bucks and weaves, dips and zooms through the warm salt air at Mission Beach - feels like an old-fashioned slice of summertime Americana. In the early 1920's, seaside amusement parks dotted the California Coast. Families would head to places like San Francisco's Playland at the Beach and L.A.'s The Pike to create memories that would blissfully linger for all time. Today, most of California's seaside amusement parks have long since been replaced with high rise condos and fancy hotels, but Belmont Shores at Mission Beach is one seaside amusement park that has managed to sidestep the currents of time and progress.

Strolling beneath the multi-hued neon sign that marks the entrance to Belmont Shores, the sweet scents of cotton candy, caramel corn, and hot dogs waft across the ocean breeze and the

cherished sounds of gleeful shrieks and laughter fill the air. Here, families can spend the entire day being rocked, rolled, plunged, swung and catapulted on rides like The Chaos, Beach Blaster, Vertical Plunge, and Giant Dipper. For families with young children, take a spin around the Carousel, chase each other on bumper cars, swim in the indoor heated pool, shop for souvenirs, and play a friendly game of air hockey at the Family Fun Arcade, then head to the ocean to master the waves on boogie boards, surfboards, skimboards and the like. If the sea is flat, no problem. Shoot the curl on the "end-less wave" at The Wave House, where ten-foot simulated tubes roll and flow like a surfer's dream.

Back on the beach, college-aged kids, libido-crazed teenagers, and marines hang out against the sea wall, watching cyclists and skaters buzz along the two-mile long boardwalk. Like a school of colorful fish, the cyclists and skaters dart left and right, ringing their bells as they pass by revelers at the oceanfront restaurants and bars. Join the party by renting a tandem bike or roller blades at any of the nearby beachside stands. Or, to find a quieter stretch, simply stroll north or south away from the crowds or on the boardwalk to the many beaches along Mission Bay.

Visit just once or a hundred times – it makes no difference – Mission Beach is one of these places so special that families call it their own. Stepping off the sidewalk and into the parking lot, the old-world charm of the 1920's era closes gently behind, but the experiences families share of roller coasters, sea breezes and saltwater taffy will remain forever.

Mission Beach's one mile of beach break is great for families with children who like to boogie board and those learning to surf. More serious surfers should head south to South Mission Jetty where there is a classic left break and a nice back door for aerial maneuvers.

Enjoy these activities and amenities while visiting Mission Beach:

Lifeguards
Surfing
Bodyboarding
Skimboarding
Bodysurfing
Swimming
Public Pool
Kite Surfing
Basketball
Amusement Park
Biking
Skateboarding
Roller Blading
Volleyball
Rentals
Restaurants
Shopping
Showers
Restrooms

Paradise Point Resort & Spa

Mission Bay

Beach Access: *Traveling south along the I-5 freeway, exit Sea World Drive/Tecolote Road. Bear right onto Sea World Drive. Exit west Mission Bay Drive. Turn left onto Quivira Road and park free in the lot.*

Traveling north along the I-5 freeway, merge onto I-8 West toward Beaches. Exit West Mission Bay Drive /Sports Arena Boulevard. Turn right onto West Mission Bay Drive. Exit onto West Mission Bay Drive. Turn left onto Quivira Road and park free in the lot.
Beach Hours: *varies from cove to cove.*

I f Mission Beach is a slice of old fashion summertime Americana, Mission Bay is the whole pie. Measuring a grand 4, 235 acres, Mission Bay is the largest man-made aquatic park in the country. Nineteen miles of sandy beaches, fourteen miles of bike paths, and a network of channels, islands, coves and wildlife preserves, offer families so many recreational activities that it's easy to spend a day, weekend or even a week on the bay. The hardest decision will be what to do first.

To get a real feel for Mission Bay, hop on a bike and pedal around the fifteen different coves and points that give this area its unique beauty. Because all of the inlets vary from

Mission Bay

one another, each trip presents itself with an endless series of discoveries. Places like Playa, Fiesta Island and De Anza Cove serve as hotspots for jet skiers, water skiers, swimmers, fishermen and over-the-line tournaments. At Mariner's Point, Perez Cove, Stoney Point, Government Island and North Fiesta Island nature lovers can witness the quiet beauty of rare and endangered birds like the California least tern and Belding's savannah sparrow. Families will enjoy picnicking, shooting hoops and playing at the playgrounds at Tecolote Shores, Crown Point and Playa.

Come sunset there is no better place to be than on the water. Rent a motorboat, kayak or sail boat and take in the view as the sun sinks below the horizon and the billowing sails shimmer in shades of violet, jade, turquoise and yellow.

Enjoy these
activities and
amenities while
visiting Mission Bay:

Lifeguards
Swimming
Windsurfing
Kayaking
Water Skiing
Jet Skiing
Sailing
Boat Rentals
Boat Ramp
Fishing
Wildlife Preserve
Bird Watching
Jogging Trails
Biking
Bike Rentals
Roller Blading
Volleyball
Basketball
Over-the-Line
Playground
Parks
Picnic Tables
Barbeques
Fire Rings
Dogs Permitted
(Fiesta Island only)
RV Camping
Hotels
Restaurants
Shopping
Showers
Restrooms

CHAPTER NINE

Ocean Beach

Dog Beach

Beach Access: *Traveling south along the I-5 freeway, exit Sea World Drive west. Stay straight to go onto Sunset Cliffs Boulevard. Turn right onto Voltaire Street.*

Traveling north along the I-5 freeway take the I-8 west toward The Beaches. Turn left onto Sunset Cliffs Boulevard, then bear right to stay on Sunset Cliffs toward the town of Ocean Beach. Turn right onto Voltaire Street. Park free in the lot and walk to the beach.
Beach Hours: *24 Hours.*

As any dog owner can attest, pups have this uncanny ability to play on human emotions. All too often, just as their owners are ready to walk out the door, book and beach towel in hand, they look up with those expressive, puppy-dog eyes and flash a desperate I-want-to-play expression. It's nearly impossible to resist. So, rather than leave the pooch behind, join hundreds of other dogs and their owners at Ocean Beach's Dog Beach where thirty-eight acres of sand, ocean, and canine companions afford dogs with the chance to run leash-free.

As an onlooker, it's a mildly crazy sight: a mad riot of dogs leaping high into the air to catch a Frisbee with their

Dog Beach

teeth, hounds dashing into the water after a ball, and a Chihuahua scurrying between a Doberman's legs to steel a treat from a stranger's hand. Surprisingly, all the dogs get along and, at the end of the day, the pets and their owners are happy to have shared the experience together.

Beyond the dogs, though, there is another side to Ocean Beach's Dog Beach. Just south of the jetty unfolds a modern "So Cal" version of the 1960's beach party. A restless mix of musicians, locals, surfers, teens, and collegians on holiday from nearby universities challenges everyone to abandon their inhibitions and indulge in the good life. A dozen or so party tents pitched along the shore house coolers filled with intoxicating delights and the sweet smoky haze from their barbecues wafts across the sand. Occasionally, locals back up their semi-trucks to the beach, unload speakers and microphones, and perform an impromptu tailgate rock concert for everyone on the strand.

Visitors find it simple to slip into the festive spirit and easily become romanced by the notion of chilling out like one of the local beach bums. Participate in a game of horseshoes, volleyball, or Frisbee, and in no time you'll be confident living the good life is the only way to live.

SURF REPORT

There are two main breaks at Dog Beach: North Jetty and Avalanches.

North Jetty, a hollow right, breaks off the south seawall of Mission Bay. Depending on the swell and tide, it can transform into a long right allowing for plenty of tricks. Best on a west swell of 2 – 8 feet.

Avalanches, located south of the jetty, is where short boarders can find good waves. Best on low tide during a big swell.

Enjoy these activities and amenities while visiting Dog Beach:

BEACH KEY

Lifeguards
Surfing
Swimming
Bodyboarding
Volleyball
Horseshoe Pits
Dogs
Bike Path
Fire Pits
Showers
Restrooms

Ocean Beach Pier

Beach Access: *Traveling along the I-5 freeway south, exit Sea World Drive toward Tecolote Road. Turn right onto Sea World Drive. Stay straight to go onto Sunset Cliffs Boulevard. Turn right onto Saratoga Avenue. Turn left onto Abbott Street. Traveling along the I-5 freeway north, merge onto the I-8 W toward beaches. Turn left onto Sunset Cliffs Boulevard. Turn right onto Saratoga Avenue. Turn left onto Abbott Street.* **Beach Hours:** *24 hours.*

Throughout California lie hidden gems: Beach towns, slightly off the beaten path, that are unique, quirky and sometimes even a bit eccentric. They are places that elicit a sense of adventure and cater to the wanderlust of travelers seeking the unexpected. San Diego's, Ocean Beach, is one such treasure. All at once laid back and lively, Ocean Beach is Hippie Central with a Punk flair.

Ocean Beach Pier

A crowded cluster of artsy shops, family-owned eateries, tattoo parlors, and open-air bars flank the Ocean Beach Pier. This is the spot to see and be seen. On any given weekend and everyday during the summer, the beach, boardwalk, and main drag –Abbott Street – are hopping. Bare-chested men and scantily clothed women, whose tattoos shine like wet ink in the glistening sun, dress up their pups in anything from doggie bathing suits to painted on pink poke-a-dots and cruise along the gritty boardwalk maneuvering between Hackey

Sac players, teens on clunky beach cruisers, and sidewalk surfers on longboard skateboards. Meanwhile, locals do drive-bys in their tricked out cars to check if the waves are pumping. Their car music, spilling out onto the street, mixes with that from the bars giving the area a pulse of its own. Invariably, the mood and music carry over onto the sand where groups of young people move to the melody while sipping on a soda or some other creative concoction.

As evening approaches, the scents of sunscreen and coconut oil still linger in the air. Surfers paddle out and fishermen cast their lines; there's no rush because the beach never closes. The perfect day lasts into the night. The axiom on one local girl's shirt sums it up perfectly, "Lucky Me".

Ocean Beach Pier draws big crowds. Beginning surfers migrate to the south side of the pier to surf the mushy lefts, while intermediate surfers head to the north side of the pier for a thick peak that peels both right and left.

Enjoy these activities and amenities while visiting Ocean Beach Pier:

Lifeguards
Surfing
Swimming
Bodyboarding
Skimboarding
Fishing
Fishing Pier
Tide Pools
Biking
Roller Blading
Shopping
Snack Bar
Restaurants
Showers
Restrooms

143

Coronado Island

Coronado City Beach

Beach Access: *Traveling north or south along the I-5 freeway, merge onto CA-75 S toward Coronado. Turn left onto Orange Avenue. Turn right onto R.H. Dana Place. R.H Dana Place becomes Ocean Boulevard. Park free in the lost by Sunset Park, or along the residential streets between Churchill Place and Ocean Drive.*
Beach Hours: *5:00am – 11:00pm*

I t's an image often seen in postcards: a gloriously large, sun washed beach with children running along the shore and the grand Hotel Del Coronado standing sentential over the strand. Coronado City Beach has the familiar feel and warmth of an endless summer. Locals tout it as a magical place: one that leads visitors far from the cares of everyday life. One local went as far as suggesting that the bridge is the magical component that transports its visitors back in time to the more carefree days of a 1920's beach community. Whether real or imagined, everyone can agree on the beach's allure.

Perhaps the most unique natural feature of this San Diego beach is the presence of patchy dunes. Like the ebb and flow of the ocean tides, these dunes have a rhythm of their own. Nature lovers will delight in seeing thousands of golden grains of sand dance and flutter across the strand, like heat shimmer, when even the gentlest of winds blow. In the spring, delicate purple verbina and yellow primrose add color to the already golden hue.

The beach itself is divided into three sections: North Beach, Central Beach, and South Beach. All cater to visitors with an abundance of sand and surf, but each offer different types of activities. North Beach, backed by Sunset Park, is an excellent place to bring the entire family, including the dog! Surf, play catch, and then head to the park for a picnic. At Central Beach enjoy swimming, bodyboarding, and volleyball. Make certain to bring a ball and net since unfortunately they are not provided. South Beach, located directly in front of the Hotel Del Coronado, features tide pools where budding scientists will have their pick of studying everything from sea anemones to sea stars.

Coronado City Beach has one major surf break, North Island. This hollow beach break is best at low tide during a clean south swell.

BEACH KEY

Enjoy these activities and amenities while visiting Coronado City Beach:

Lifeguards
Surfing
Swimming
Bodysurfing
Bodyboarding
Skimboarding
Fishing
Tidepools
Volleyball
Kite Flying
Fire Rings
Park
Picnic Tables
Restrooms
Showers
Dogs Permitted
(North Beach)

Coronado Shores

Beach Access: *Traveling north or south along the I-5 freeway, exit onto CA-75 toward Coronado. Continue on Pomona Ave. Turn left onto 3rd Street. Turn left onto Orange Ave. Park free in the lot by the Coronado Shores condo complex or along the street and walk to the beach.*
Beach Hours: *5:00am – 11:00pm*

From the bow of the Coronado Commuter ferry, Coronado Shores beach looks like a Monet painting where every brush stroke is thoughtfully placed. As the boat motors closer, the community takes on a three dimensional form: a golden beach strand edged by the deep blue Pacific, high-rise condos, and the opulent Hotel Del Coronado. It's an illustrious vision, storybook beautiful and reminiscent of the legendary city of gold, El Dorado.

Coronado Shores

But beyond the beauty lies a fascinating past. The island's history dates back almost four-hundred years ago to the days of the Spanish explorer, Sebastian Vizcaino. In 1602, he and his expedition party caught sight of the Islands and named them Las Yslas Coronadas, from which its current name, Coronado Island, is derived. Fast forward some two hundred years to the era of Mexican land grants. Governor Pio Pico deeded Coronado and her sister island, North Island to Don Pedro Carrillo. He used the land for a short period of time as a grazing pasture for cattle, then quite hastily, sold the islands for a meager $1,000. Over the next 49 years, the island changed hands many times. Eventually, in 1885 Elisha S. Babcock, Jr., Hampton L. Story, and Jacob Gruendike purchased the property for $100,000. Their goal was to create a grand seaside resort community, complete with a magnificent hotel. Today, all those who visit Coronado Island can appreciate their vision and find it to be just as spectacular as the city founders intended.

Coronado Shores steals the hearts of all who visit. It simultaneously offers both the feeling of tranquility and the comforts of civilization. Perhaps, the best way to enjoy Coronado Shores is to breakfast at the hotel's Sunday brunch then stroll along the beach or bike along the board-walk. At the end of the day, watch as the sun melts into the ocean, turning the water's edge into a golden vision.

The waves at
Coronado Shores
are generally smaller
than the waves at other
San Diego beaches. Catch
it on a clean south swell
though and you'll find
some awesome hollow
surf. Along the north end
of the beach, surf the slow
peeling right that breaks
off the jetty.

SURF REPORT

**Enjoy these activities
and amenities while
visiting Coronado
Shores:**

Lifeguards
Surfing
Swimming
Skimboarding
Bodyboarding
Volleyball
Rentals
Bike Path
Restaurant
Hotels

BEACH KEY

151

Silver Strand State Beach

Beach Access: *Traveling south along the I-5 freeway, exit CA-75 toward Coronado. Cross over the bridge, and then turn left onto Orange Avenue. Orange Avenue becomes Silver Strand Boulevard. Exit Coronado Cays Boulevard and turn right into the State Park.*

Traveling north along the I-5 freeway, exit Palm Avenue, west. Turn onto Silver Strand Boulevard/Highway 75 and exit Coronado Cays Boulevard. Turn west and continue into the State Beach.

Beach Hours: *8:00am – 9:00pm*

Camping Reservations: ***www.reserveamerica.com***

W hat exactly goes into making the perfect California getaway? For many beach-loving families the formula is simple: great surf, miles of soft white sand, maybe a bike path nearby, plus a campground for when everyone is simply having too much fun to leave.

Traveling south along highway 75 brings visitors past the charming city of Coronado to Silver Strand State Beach, a surprising likable isthmus on a remote corner of this small island. At first glance, Silver Strand appears more like a cement monstrosity than a family beach destination. With its 2,000 parking spaces and 130 campsites - sporting

apartment-sized RV's - many travelers' initial response is to keep driving. But, for those who do decide to stop, they will discover that Silver Strand is one of those special places where families can get away from it all and still find plenty to do.

The absence of modern stores and fast-food restaurants means that life centers around the beach. With two-and-a-half miles of ocean strand, one-half mile of bay-front beach, a nature preserve, and nearly twenty activities ranging from in-line skating to water skiing, Silver Strand features a full complement of amusements to entertain even the choosiest of families.

On the other hand, many find it irresistible to adapt to the unhurried pace of island life and simply delight in the sweetness of doing nothing – idling away the days sprawled out on a beach chair, nibbling on fruit, and sipping champagne.

NO LIFEGUARD ON DUTY

Silver Strand's beach break comes to life summer and fall when the south and south swells hit SoCal. Being a fully exposed beach, steady side onshore and side-shore winds make this beach great for kite surfing.

Enjoy these activities and amenities while visiting Silver Strand State Beach:

Lifeguards
Surfing
Bodyboarding
Swimming
Boating
Water Skiing
Jet Skiing
Volleyball
Fishing
Fire Rings
Bike Path
R.V. Camping
Barbecues
Picnic Tables
Nature Preserve
Bird Watching
Dogs Permitted
(allowed only in camping area)
SBC FreedomLink™ Service
Snack Bar
Rentals
Showers
Restrooms
Parking Fee

155

Imperial Beach Pier

Beach Access: *Traveling north or south along the I-5 freeway exit Palm Avenue. Turn left onto Seacoast Drive. Continue straight on Seacoast Drive and park free along the street or in the metered parking lot.*
Beach Hours: *5:00pm – 10:00pm.*

Fishing from a rustic wooden pier, constructing castles out of sand, gourmet ice-cream, bric-a-brac shops, the salt-scented Pacific, and surfing – it's "Classic Southern California" at its best. Imperial Beach remains one of the last Southern California coastal cities that has managed to maintain an uncrowded, small-town feel. Thanks to an ordinance established in the 1970's that banned high-rise development, visitors have the chance to experience a timeless piece of coastal Southern California.

The entrance to the beach and pier is through a sculpted archway, which features a set of cascading waves in lipstick pink, lime green, flitter gold, and purple. The words, sprawled

across the top, "Imperial Beach", shimmer in the sun. It's a virtual kaleidoscope of color and picture perfect with palm trees, a grassy green park and pier in the background.

A standout spot long known to avid fisherman, The Imperial Beach Pier stretches 1500 feet from end to end. Join the locals out on the center of the pier and cast a baited line past the pilings where what seems like a thousand silvery fish swim lazily below. With any luck, the line will begin to sing as a fat pile perch or rubberlip seaperch runs with the bait. In the event the fish takes off with the bait, don't be discouraged, simply stroll down to the end of the pier at the Tin Fish Restaurant and dine on fresh seafood that someone else was lucky enough to catch.

Back on the strand, enjoy Imperial Beach's favorite pastime: sandcastle building. Home to the renown U.S. Open Sandcastle Competition, this beach is known to have some of the best sand for constructing not only castles but veritable cities. Visit during Sandcastle Weekend and enjoy a Friday night sandcastle ball, Saturday street festival with a pancake breakfast, street vendors, parade, children's rides, arts and crafts, musical entertainment, firework display and Kids-N-Kastles contest. Come back on Sunday for the official U.S. Open Sandcastle Competition where skilled sand artists compete for the Master's Champion title and over $21,000 in cash prizes. Check the city's official website for specific dates and times. *(http://www.cityofib.com)*

There are two great spots to fish at Imperial Beach: The pier and just behind the surf line. Fishing from the pier is easy and free. You don't need a fishing license to fish off the pier. Just drop your line off the middle or end and wait to reel in any–thing from croaker and queenfish to walleye surfperch, jacksmelt, halibut, sand sharks and guitarfish.

Fishing from the shore requires a fishing license, but this is the best place to catch barred surfperch, California corbina, yellowfin or spotfin croaker. Scoop up sand crabs or pry mussels from the pier pilings and use them as bait, then cast out into the surf and sit back and wait.

Enjoy these activities and amenities while visiting Imperial Beach Pier:

BEACH KEY

Lifeguards
Surfing
Swimming
Bodyboarding
Skimboarding
Surf Fishing
Fishing Pier
Sand Castle Building
Shopping
Restaurants
Park
Playground
Basketball
Volleyball
Picnic Tables
Showers
Restrooms
Handicap Facilities
Parking Fee

Border Field State Park

Beach Access: *Traveling north or south along the I-5 freeway, exit Dairy Mart Road. After several miles, turn right onto Monument Road. Continue through the gate if the kiosk is attended, otherwise park in the lot at the kiosk and follow the dirt road to the beach.*
Beach Hours: *Wednesday through Sunday, 10:00 am to 5:00 pm*

Driving along Dairy Mart Road, visitors to Border Field State Park may feel as though they have left the United States altogether and are now driving down an obscure, rutted path somewhere in Mexico. Just a few miles north, this side of the Mexican boarder, San Diego's modern metropolis and cosmopolitan buildings give way to horse ranches and small houses in various states of ruin, preservation, or restoration. Vaqueros (Mexican cowboys) riding on horseback, who seem to have traded in the city's fast pace lifestyle for a carefree, "no problema, I'll do it mañana existence", tip their hats and smile at passersby on the way to the park.

Border Field State Park

Border Field State Park is part of the Tijuana Estuary, a 2,500-acre reserve dedicated to education and research. With only 10% of Southern California's coastal wetland habitat remaining – 90% has been lost to development – Tijuana Estuary is an excellent place to see indigenous estuarine flora and fauna firsthand. Join docents on a nature or bird walk on any weekend to learn about the natural history of the area and to see a variety of resident and migratory birds that use the estuary as a breeding, feeding, and nesting place or as a stopover while traveling along the Pacific Flyway. Also offered at the park is Junior Ranchers program, where children 7- 12 years of age participate in maintaining a native plant garden, viewing wildlife, and doing arts and crafts. The park also features a Speaker Series, where once a month biologists, specialists or researchers lecture on estuary-related topics. Equestrian trails are located throughout the park and provide horse lovers with a unique opportunity to not only ride through eight different habitats, but also run their colts along the beach strand. Horse rentals are available at nearby stables.

As the southern most beach in California, Border Field has two severe drawbacks. First, the ocean is sometimes polluted due to sewage-contaminated plumes from the Tijuana Estuary. Swimming is not recommended. Second, while walking along a desolate, pristine strand- where yours are likely to be the only footprints- is usually a tranquil experience, here, all too often, beachgoers will be startled back into reality by the green and white border patrol jeeps, spitting sand from their wheels, as they scream past with their sirens blaring. It's reminiscent of a drug-bust scene in some action packed movie. For the most part, those who visit Border Field State Park are horseback riders or Mexican -American residents who make their way down to the international boarder to talk with friends and family through the fence.

Throughout the year Border Field State Park hosts special events that center on ecology, conservation, and the history of the Tijuana River Estuary. Bring the family and join in the celebrations with docent-led bird and nature walks, presentations, arts and crafts, maintaining and improving a native plant garden, beach and waterway cleanups, and live stories, music, dance, and drama of the peoples that lived near the Tijuana River Estuary since pre-historic times. Contact the visitor center for specific dates and times. Phone: (619) 575-3613 www.tijuanaestuary.com.

Enjoy these activities and amenities while visiting Border Field State Beach:

Hiking Trials
Equestrian Trails
Bird Watching
Interpretive Programs
Restrooms
Parking Fee

Recommendations

101 Café

631 South Coast Highway
Oceanside, CA 92054
telephone: (760) 722-5220
web: **www.101cafe.net**

Great food. Fun atmosphere. Historical photos. Located on Historic Highway 101. The 101 Café, established in 1928 as a

20-seat diner, is the West Coast's oldest and best café on the Historic Highway 101. Eating at the Café will be an experience you will long remember. Open everyday except Christmas 6:30 am till Midnight.

Canes Bar & Grill

3105 Ocean Front Walk
San Diego, CA 92109
telephone: (858) 488-1780
web: **www.canesbarandgrill.com**

Canes Bar & Grill is San Diego's hidden hot spot, located directly on the ocean in beautiful Mission Beach. With a unique oceanfront restaurant and rooftop deck, Canes is the perfect place to dine or enjoy a famous Hurricane drink. The nightclub

features live national and local talent. The San Diego Reader calls Canes "One of the best live music venues in town." Happy Hour Monday - Friday from 5:00 p.m. till sunset. Also, for sports fans, Canes has 25 satellite-ready televisions for your game-watching enjoyment.

Chart House

2588 South Coast Hwy 101
Cardiff, CA 92007
telephone: (760) 436-4044
web: **www.chart-house.com**

You'll have a front row seat to crashing waves and panoramic Southern California sunsets at this magnificent oceanfront Chart House. From top-of-the-catch seafood, succulent steaks and decadent

desserts, Chart House's renowned chefs have tailored a menu to complement local cuisine while introducing a hint of the exotic. Choose from famous entrées such as Snapper Hemingway, Shrimp Fresca and their slow roasted Prime Rib. They also offer a daily selection of fresh fish, an extensive collection of fine wines and whiskies, and decadent desserts, like their famous Hot Chocolate Lava Cake.

En Fuego Cantina & Grill

141 Camino del Mar
Del Mar, CA 92014
telephone: (858) 792-6551
web: **www.enfuegocantina.com**

The En Fuego Cantina & Grill locale has long been known for serving traditional Mexican dishes and fresh seafood. With the help of Chef Todd Castner, they have been able to add to that legacy; their specials exemplify "South of the Border" cuisine from Mexico through South America. Enjoy Happy Hour everyday from 4:30pm – 6:30pm and Tuesday Night Tacos 4:30pm until close.

Georges At The Cove

1250 Prospect Street
La Jolla, CA 92037
telephone: (858) 454-4244
web: **www.georgesatthecove.com**

Three distinct dining experiences with spectacular ocean views await at Georges At The Cove in La Jolla Village: Georges California Modern, Ocean Terrace and

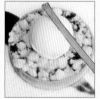

George's Bar. An all-new upscale contemporary restaurant and bar, Georges California Modern offers a sophisticated but relaxed indoor environment featuring California cuisine prepared with fresh, local, and seasonal ingredients. For a more casual bistro menu, try the Ocean Terrace whose rooftop dining is next to none. George's Bar delights diners with signature cocktails and panoramic views of La Jolla Cove.

Jakes Del Mar *On the Sand in Del Mar*

1660 Coast Boulevard
Del Mar, CA 92014
telephone: (858) 755-2002
web: **www.jakesdelmar.com**

Come and tease the ocean. Floor-to-ceiling windows provide dramatic views of the Pacific, and Jakes proximity to the water lets you sit just out of reach of the tide. Their inviting ambiance along with genuine, friendly service makes for a casual atmosphere and a favorite among locals and visitors alike. Their menu showcases California coastal cuisine featuring fresh fish, and a variety of shellfish along with premium steaks and chops.

Molly's Restaurant & Wine Bar

333 West Harbor Drive
San Diego, CA 92101
telephone: (619) 230-8909
web: **www.mollysfinedining.com**

A celebration of New American cuisine, the farm comes to the table nightly at Molly's Restaurant & Wine Bar located in

the heart of downtown San Diego at the San Diego Marriott Hotel and Marina.

Delighting diners with an innovative seasonal menu featuring fresh, artisan grown products from small local and regional farms, an extensive, award-winning wine list expertly crafted by Wine Director and Sommelier Lisa Redwine showcasing a range of varietals and vineyards, and a level of service rarely seen in San Diego. The dining concept at Molly's is simple – use the freshest ingredients from area farms and artisan purveyors to create food that is clean and flavorful. Behind the culinary vision at Molly's is Chef Timothy Au whose menu changes nightly, always reflecting the seasonality and availability of seafood, meats and vegetables. Au joined the staff at Molly's Restaurant in September of 2007 after spending two years as the executive chef at the Five-Star and Five-Diamond Mayflower Inn & Spa in Washington, Connecticut. Please call for reservations: (619) 230-8909

The Marine Room

2000 Spindrift Dr
La Jolla, CA 92037
telephone: (858) 459-7222
web: **www.marineroom.com**

Opened in 1941, the multi-award winning Marine Room Restaurant's spectacular ocean views, exemplary service, and wine list makes it San Diego's premier dining destination. Experience a culinary journey as you indulge in global cuisine rooted in the French classics. Located along the shores of La Jolla, enjoy the ocean tide just inches from your window. More than great dining, The Marine Room is a tradition not to be missed.

Vigilucci's Seafood & Steakhouse

3878 Carlsbad Boulevard
Carlsbad, CA 92008
telephone: (760) 434-2580
web: **www.vigiluccis.com**

Located directly across from the tranquil waves of the Pacific Ocean, enjoy breathtaking views of the evening sunset while enjoying some of the most exquisite cuisine in North County. The menu features only certified prime steaks and the freshest seafood, all with a signature Italian flair and paired with an award-winning wine list.

Restaurants

Accommodations

Best Western Encinitas Inn & Suites
85 Encinitas Boulevard
Encinitas, CA 92024
telephone: (760) 942-7455
web: **www.bwencinitas.com**

Encinitas Inn & Suites, situated atop the bluffs in Encinitas, overlooks picturesque Moonlight State Beach. With meeting facilities and conference services, plus nearby attractions, such as The Carlsbad Flower Fields, Legoland, Birch Aquarium, and San Diego Zoo, Encinitas Inn & Suites is ideal for both business or pleasure. Newly renovated, this full-service hotel features deluxe suites with a Jacuzzi and kitchenette or oversized guest rooms with a balcony and ocean view. Complimentary, deluxe Continental breakfast, ocean view rooms, outdoor heated pool and whirlpool.

El Cordova Hotel
1351 Orange Avenue
Coronado, CA 92118
telephone: (619) 435-4131
web: **www.elcordovahotel.com**

This charming "Spanish village" hotel, originally built as a countryside mansion for Elisha Babcock in 1902, was later converted into a lovely hotel offering its guests friendly and informal surroundings

with attentive staff to ensure a wonderful stay. Only one block to the world's most beautiful beach and Glorietta Bay, the El Cordova Hotel is located in the heart of Coronado, close to shops, theatres and a vast variety of recreational opportunities. Individually designed rooms and suites at the El Cordova Hotel offer cable TV with premium channels and high-speed Internet access. El Cordova Hotel on Coronado Island features 3 restaurants, 20 boutiques and a courtyard with heated pool & spa tub.

Glorietta Bay Inn
1630 Glorietta Boulevard
Coronado, CA 92118
telephone: (619) 435-3101
web: **www.gloriettabayinn.com**

Coronado's Best Kept Secret!

Step back in time, and enjoy the charm of this beautiful 100-year-old mansion. Overlooking San Diego's scenic Glorietta Bay and one block from the Pacific Ocean, sits Coronado landmark, Glorietta Bay Inn.

Combining old world charm with contemporary comfort, the inn is comprised of an 11-room bed-and-breakfast and 89 rooms in the contemporary buildings surrounding the mansion. The inn features a variety of room types from standard rooms to family suites to upscale mansion bedrooms. Enjoy complimentary continental breakfast, afternoon refreshments and heated pool and spa.

Hilton San Diego Resort & Spa
1775 E. Mission Bay Drive
San Diego, CA 92109
telephone: (619) 276-4010
web: **www.sandiegohilton.com**

With its picture-perfect bays, year-round sunshine and world-class tourist attractions, San Diego makes an ideal getaway destination. And with a prime, bay front position on beautiful Mission Bay, the Hilton San Diego Resort is the perfect spot for a holiday. This Four-Diamond beach resort is conveniently located one

mile from SeaWorld. A romantic paradise of palms, perfect sandy bay fronts, this bayside retreat is complete with an all-new $5 million dollar crown jewel, Essence - the Spa on Mission Bay and state of the art fitness center, beautifully refreshed guestrooms, plus Concerts on the Bay and a host of other sunshiny events.

Hotel Del Coronado
1500 Orange Avenue
Coronado, CA 92118
telephone: (800) HOTELDEL
web: **www.hoteldel.com**

Rising from the water's edge on the quaint island of Coronado in San Diego, the Hotel del Coronado is considered one of America's most beautiful beach resorts. A classic historic hotel, The Del was built in 1888 and designated a National Historic Landmark in 1977. Today, The Del offers travelers contemporary luxury in an enchanting Victorian atmosphere. The Del offers a quintessential San Diego resort vacation experience for those seeking a family vacation destination, romantic retreat, or business trip.

Manchester Grand Hyatt
One Market Place
San Diego, CA 92101
telephone: (619) 232-1234
web: **www.manchestergrand.hyatt.com**

The Manchester Grand Hyatt San Diego is a luxurious waterfront urban hotel and spa with 1,625 luxury bay and city view rooms, including 95 suites just steps from Seaport Village, Petco Park and the exciting nightlife of the Gaslamp Quarter. Located on the San Diego Bay, this urban resort showcases two pools, full service spa and fitness center and a selection of restaurants and lounges; including Top of the Hyatt, voted "Best Upscale Bar" in San Diego.

Pacific Terrace Hotel
610 Diamond Street
San Diego CA 92109
telephone: (800) 344-3370
web: **www.pacificterrace.com**

Pacific Terrace Hotel - San Diego's hidden gem...
Overlooking the white sandy beaches of San Diego, the Pacific Terrace Hotel offers spectacular views of the Pacific Ocean. 73 Guest rooms & suites feature a 'Tommy Bahama' motif to enhance the island feel. This AAA 4 Diamond awarded hotel in Pacific Beach, California stands between the sun and the surf, midway between Mission Bay and La Jolla, and strikes the perfect balance between comfort and luxury, serenity and inspiration.

West Inn & Suites
4970 Avenida Encinas
Carlsbad, CA 92008
telephone: (866) 431-9378
web: **www.westinnsuites.com**

West Inn & Suites is a boutique style hotel that offers the ultimate in luxurious surroundings and recreational activities. Their brand-new property has a resort like atmosphere and features upgraded amenities and unrivaled service. Just 30 miles north of San Diego and 55 miles south of Los Angeles/Orange County, The West Inn & Suites has is an ideal location for both the business and recreational traveler. The West Inn & Suites has 86 luxurious rooms including 36 suites, a fine dining restaurant, fitness center, outdoor heated pool and Jacuzzi, business center, boardroom and library.

BajaSail.Net

Day Sailing • Sunset Cruises • Private Parties
Oceanside, CA 92054

telephone: (760) 613-9384
web: **www.Bajasail.net**

Experience the thrill of wind-fueled travel on a large 36-foot Catamaran, that accommodates up to 6 passengers. Actively learn to sail the boat, or simply put your feet up, loosen your shoulders and enjoy the oceans breeze. Daily operation from Oceanside Harbor. The trips sail along the coast, always within site of land. Fully crewed with a licensed captain and crewmember. Charter of the entire boat is also available for private parties.

Bob's Mission Surf Shop

4320 Mission Blvd.
San Diego, CA 92109
telephone: (858) 483-8837
web: **www.missionsurf.com**

Repair • Rentals • Lessons • Sales
Long Boards • Short Boards • Body Boards
Fins and Stand Up Paddle Surfing

When Bob's Mission Surf opened in 1993, it was their goal to have a surf shop like the kind from the 60's; a shop that was a fun place to hang out, see new products and check out the coolest surfboards in town. They wanted to be able to offer services and expert assistance to seasoned surfers as well as those who were just getting their feet wet. Today, their shop reflects not only those goals but also embraces the values and traditions of those long ago years when the surf shop was the hub of the surfing community.

Eli Howard Surf School

P.O. Box 232690
Encinitas, CA 92023
telephone: (760) 809-3069
web: **www.elihoward.com**

We live for surf, and have shared our passion for surfing with thousands of people since 1999. our surfing lessons and camps are conducted with a professional, hands-on, and supportive style that is second to none. Daily surfing lessons, day surf camps, parties and special events, weekend overnight camping.

Hansen Surfboards

1105 S Coast Highway 101
Encinitas, CA 92024
telephone: (760) 753-6595
web: **www.hansensurf.com**

Hansen's single location in Encinitas is the largest surf shop in San Diego County! 16,000 square feet of retail space gives them the unique ability to offer something for everyone in the family, both young and old. They have apparel, beach accessories, surf gear, snow gear, skate gear and even home décor! Talk about a one-stop shop!

Activities

La Jolla Kayak

Kayak and Bike Tours & Rentals!

2199 Avenida de la Playa
La Jolla, CA 92037
telephone: (858) 459-1114
web: www.lajollakayak.com

La Jolla Kayak, operating since 1995, offers an extraordinary way to discover La Jolla's spectacular seven caves and underwater park with the Original Kayak tour. Their experienced staff can help you experience the natural beauty of La Jolla Shores with guided Leopard shark

snorkel tours or whale watching by kayak. The Soledad Slide bike tour is an awe-inspiring ride through La Jolla's famous scenery. La Jolla Kayak rents single or double kayaks, surfboards, boogie boards and snorkeling equipment for those that want to explore on their own along with their guided tours. Experience the beauty and adventure of the Southern California coastline and come away with a new appreciation for the dramatic beauty of the ocean environment at Jolla Kayak.

Leucadia Surf boards

1144 North Coast Highway 101
Encinitas, CA 92024
telephone: (760) 632-1010

This classic California surf shop features a

nice selection of boards, wetsuits and surf paraphernalia, board rentals, wetsuits, surf gear and clothing.

Seaforth Boat Rentals

1641 Quivira Road
San Diego, CA 92109
telephone: (619) 223-1681

web: www.seaforthboatrental.com
   www.SBRwakeboarding.com

Seaforth Boat Rentals invites you to enjoy San Diego at its BEST! With a fleet of over 200 boats and locations in Mission Bay, Coronado and Downtown San Diego, since 1975 we have had the local waterways covered! We are the largest and most modern boat rental company in Southern

California. Whether you are looking to sail, paddle, fish, jetski, wakeboard or just cruise in a powerboat, we have the perfect boat for you. Enjoy the San Diego skyline, playful sealions, historic sights and awesome aircraft carriers, all from the water.

Surf Zone

1009 North Coast Highway
Oceanside, CA 92054
telephone: (760) 722-1295

Oceanside's premier surf shop. Check out our wide selection of surfboards, clothing and gear than head to the beach just a few blocks away.

Team Wahine Surfing School

telephone: (760) 445-5331
web: www.teamwahine.com
web: www.alohanuihula.com

Learn to surf with Team Wahine Surfing School at Oceanside's Harbor Beach. Team Wahine offers private surf lessons, 5 day surf camps with a 3:1 ratio of students to instructors, hourly rentals, apparel, beach and surf products as well as keepsakes from Hawaii, Tahiti and Indonesia. The Wahine is Oceanside's Home Town Gidget.

The Wave House

3125 Ocean Front Walk
San Diego, CA 92109
telephone: (858) 228-WAVE (228-9283)
web: www.wavehouse.com

Whether you surf, skate, or snowboard, novice or pro, The Wave House's simulated surf platforms let you hone your skills on endless waves. Eat, Drink and be Merry in a White Sand Village Oasis with outdoor

Tiki bars, open-air barbecues, fire pits, hammocks, tropical palms and meandering boardwalks. After a tough day in the surf, catch the sunset from the Windansea Bar, enjoy a cold cerveza, and talk story about your wave of the day.

Birch Aquarium at Scripps
2300 Expedition Way
La Jolla, CA 92093-0207
telephone: (858) 534-FISH
web: **www.aquarium.ucsd.edu/**

Explore Birch Aquarium at Scripps, where the wonders of the ocean come alive! View a stunning variety of colorful, Pacific marine life featured in more than 60 habitats. Interact with hands-on exhibits that showcase cutting-edge research discoveries that have profound impacts on what we know about Earth's systems and how these discoveries are relevant to our everyday lives. Explore outdoor tide pools where you can touch and learn about the spectacular animals that live in these ecosystems.

   As the public exploration center for world-renowned Scripps Institution of Oceanography at UC San Diego, Birch Aquarium has inspired San Diego's residents and visitors with the wonders of the ocean for more than a century. Since 1903, Scripps Institution of Oceanography has maintained an aquarium and museum dedicated to public education and enjoyment. Birch Aquarium at Scripps is a heartwarming and memorable experience for people of all ages. Open daily 9 a.m. to 5 p.m.

California Welcome Center – Oceanside
928 North Coast Highway
Oceanside, CA 92054
telephone: (760) 721-1101
toll free: (800) 350-7873
web: **www.visitoceanside.org**

Find yourself here, literally…the California Welcome Center provides local, regional and state tourist information and maps. From brochures on San Diego's famous attractions to hidden treasures off the beaten path, there is a plethora of information available to suit everyone's taste and budget. The Center's loyal staff and volunteers welcome thousands of visitors every year. Their local knowledge and passion for our region ensures every visitor need is met with enthusiasm. With just one stop, visitors can purchase discount tickets to major attractions, make hotel reservations, purchase the perfect California keepsake or even take a breather. The California Welcome Center in Oceanside is one of the Official Sate Visitor Centers. We are here as your personal travel concierge to assist you with every aspect of your California experience. Conveniently located at the gateway to San Diego.

Bay Books
1029 Orange Avenue
Coronado, CA 92118
Phone: (619) 435-0075
web: **www.baybookscoronado.com**

San Diego's largest independent bookstore, located on beautiful Coronado Island, boasts a wide selection of books for children, military history books, international magazines, foreign language books and books on tape.

Bwarie Gift Basket Company
300 Carlsbad Village Drive • #104
Carlsbad, CA 92008
Phone: (858) 483-8837
telephone: (760) 730-1456
web: **www.bwariegiftbaskets.com**

Exclusive, Handcrafted **Gift Baskets**

The ultimate gift for all occasions is a gift basket from Bwarie Gift Basket Company. From client appreciation gifts to special

events for family and friends, you will find the perfect gift at The Bwarie Gift Basket Company, where each gift basket is personally handcrafted with fun and unique items. Shipping is available throughout the United States. Engraving on wine bottles at no charge.

Detour Salon & Store

594 S. Coast Hwy 101
Encinitas, CA 92024
telephone: (760) 634-1999
web: **www.detoursalon.com**

Detour Salon and Store have become THE destination in North County for style and lifestyle. Detour stylists meet today's demand for quality, expressive hair design with mastery of both trendy and classic cutting and coloring techniques. Detour the Store offers the entire Bumble & Bumble™ range of care and styling products, as well as exclusive fashion-forward apparel, eclectic accessories, books, and other intriguing items. At Detour, beauty is fun and life is a beautiful adventure. We're proud of our healthy culture – the collective attitudes of our multi-generational staff and customers. Grace & integrity are who we are and what we offer.

Paper Rose

705 North Vulcan Avenue
Encinitas, CA 92024
telephone: (760) 436-2855
web: **www.paperrosegifts.com**

Not just a store, a destination! Relax in our beautiful garden in our dog friendly "Moon Mania Doggy Café" and enjoy free coffee and tea while indulging in a tasty treat for you and  your four-legged friend. Browse and shop in our charming cottage store for unique cards, gifts, stationary, chocolates and works by local artists.

Paradise Cove

4500 Ocean Blvd.
San Diego, CA 92109
telephone: (858) 272-1407
web: **www.sandiegocandlefactory.com**

Paradise Cove is located right on the beach at the entrance to Crystal Pier. Here you will find a wide selection of beachwear, headwear, gifts and everything that you  need for a day at the beach. We also feature a wide selection of shells from around the world and beautiful seashell candles made right here in San Diego.

Queen Eileen's

548 South Coast Highway.
Encinitas, CA 92024
telephone: (760) 436-4845
web: **www.queeneileens.com**

A fun shop filled with anything you could possibly need or want, as long as you have a sense of humor. Beach themed gifts, Old Guys Rule T-shirts and hats, lots of girlfriend gifts, tons of jewelry, retro toys for kids and much, much more.

Upstart Crow

835 C West Harbor Drive
San Diego, CA 92101
telephone: (619) 232-4855
web: **www.upstartcrowtrading.com**

Upstart Crow Bookstore and Coffeehouse has been a highlight of Seaport Village in downtown San Diego for over twenty years. Located right on the beautiful San Diego Bay, the shop has a unique and eclectic selection of books, gifts, cards, paper goods, and gourmet delights. Select from a tempting menu of fabulous desserts and truly fine coffees. Rarely, will you find such an interesting and clever mixture of merchandise in such a comfortable setting. Enjoy the relaxing ambiance of the tables in the upstairs loft or sit on the outdoor patio and enjoy the cool evening breezes off the bay. The shop is open seven days a week, from 9:00 am to 9:00pm, every day of the year. Talented local musicians provide live music every Saturday night. Named for William Shakespeare, the Upstart Crow will definitely provide many pleasant hours of entertainment.

Index

Order Form

SUN, SAND & SURF

The Ultimate Guide To Orange County Beaches

Quantity	Book Price	Shipping & Handling	Subtotal
	$27.50	$8.00	
California residents please add 7.75% sales tax per book.			
Total			

The Beaches of SAN DIEGO

Your Ultimate Guide to the Sun, Sand and Surf

Quantity	Book Price	Shipping & Handling	Subtotal
	$29.50	$8.00	
California residents please add 7.75% sales tax per book.			
Total			

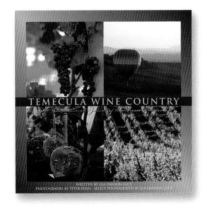

TEMECULA WINE COUNTRY
The Undiscovered Jewel of Southern California

Quantity	Book Price	Shipping & Handling	Subtotal
	$27.50	$8.00	
California residents please add 7.75% sales tax per book.			
Total			

Please send check or money order to:
Vista Pacifica Publishing Company
P.O. Box 373 • Dana Point, CA 92629-0373
telephone: (949) 395-2878 • e-mail: vistapacifica1@cox.net

Redeemable For One Complimentary 7 Caves Kayak Tour

La Jolla Kayak

Kayak and Bike Tours & Rentals!

Redeemable for one complimentary 7 Caves Kayak Tour when the bearer buys the first tour at regular price. Compliments of Vista Pacifica Publishing Company and La Jolla Kayak.

Please see reverse side for valid requirements and restrictions.

For reservations call **(858) 459-1114** or visit **www.lajollakayak.com**

Void if electronically copied, scanned, or altered.

Redeemable For One Sailing Cruise Along The San Diego Coast

Private Charters
Sunset Cruises
Day Sailing

Redeemable for one complimentary sailing cruise when the bearer buys the first sailing cruise at regular price. Compliments of Vista Pacifica Publishing Company and Baja Sail.

Please see reverse side for valid requirements and restrictions.

For reservations call **(760) 613-9384** or visit **www.bajasail.net**

Void if electronically copied, scanned, or altered.

La Jolla Kayak

Kayak and Bike Tours & Rentals!

La Jolla Kayak should complete this section when the certificate is redeemed. Mail completed certificate to: Vista Pacifica Publishing, Company P.O. Box 373, Dana Point, CA 92629

Name of Guest
_____

Home Address
_____

City _____ State _____ Zip _____

Telephone Number
_____

Signature
_____

Certificate is good for one complimentary 7 Cave Kayak Tour with the purchase of one 7 Cave Kayak Tour at the regular price. Subject to availability. Advanced reservations recommended. Restrictions apply. Vista Pacifica Publishing Company is not responsible for any changes in individual kayak tour operation or policy. By use of this certificate, consumer agrees to release Vista Pacifica Publishing Company from any liability in connection with their travel to and touring with La Jolla Kayak. This certificate may not be reproduced and cannot be used in conjunction with any other promotional offers. Void where prohibited. Void if electronically copied, scanned or altered.

Private Charters • Sunset Cruises • Day Sailing

BajaSail.net completes this section when the certificate is redeemed. Mail completed certificate to: Vista Pacifica Publishing, Company P.O. Box 373, Dana Point, Ca 92629

Name of Guest
_____

Home Address
_____

City _____ State _____ Zip _____

Telephone Number
_____

Signature
_____

Certificate is good for one complimentary sailing cruise with the purchase of one sailing cruise at the regular price. Subject to availability. Advanced reservations recommended. Restrictions apply. Vista Pacifica Publishing Company is not responsible for any changes in individual sailing tour operation or policy. By use of this certificate, consumer agrees to release Vista Pacifica Publishing Company from any liability in connection with their travel to and sailing with BajaSail.net. This certificate may not be reproduced and cannot be used in conjunction with any other promotional offers. Void where prohibited. Void if electronically copied, scanned or altered.

Please remove gift certificates along perforated score.